OF COURSE, **UNDREAMED**

AMEN MOHAMMED

A MEMOIR

Acknowledgments

I thank my son, Obama H. Shibo, who was with me up and down roads and helped us survive by babysitting himself at that young age when I went to driving. I thank my husband, Aman T. Tuke, who has supported me since our relationship, trusts me in every step I go, and keeps me moving from behind in my journey and accomplishments. I thank my English teacher Michele Hampton, who told me I could write a book and made me confident about writing. Thanks to my editor Yasmin G who did a great editing job. Thanks to OAFRICA VIRTUAL COLLEGE FOR GRAPHIC DESIGN for doing the graphics and designing my book. Thanks to Mr. Hamza Wariyo who gave me advice and comments on the book and encouraged me. I thank Mr. Hussein Abbas Hajii, who did the formatting. A final Big thanks to Prof. Abbas Gnamo, who read my book thoroughly and gave me comments to correct any errors and gave me forewords.

Foreword

As the saying goes, "Life is not a bed of roses," this is particularly true for immigrants who come to a new country, new culture, new climate, and a way of life. Surviving, adjusting, and thriving are not given. It is full of ups and downs, times of hope, despair, and uncertainties. Only resilient and hardworking people can navigate troubled waters to realize their dreams. This is exemplified by a book entitled "*Of Course Undreamed,*" authored by Amen Mohammad, an Oromo woman who migrated and settled in the United States a decade ago. This beautifully written and narrated personal story starts with her family background: she was born in Asasa, in a large Arsii Oromo family, and, as such, has dozens of brothers and sisters. She received substantial education back home, where she worked as a journalist while studying Law at the same time. Suddenly, she won a DV lottery to migrate to the United States and contemplated the American dream. The dream was higher than ever at the time when Barack Obama was the president of the United States. Barack Obama, the first African American president, was known for his motivational slogan 'yes we can'; she appears to have been inspired by this motto and said to herself, "Yes, I can," which may be why she named her son after Obama. Her well-being has constituted the primary focus of her daily concerns and life.

The book, divided into ten chronologically organized chapters, vividly narrates her experience and daily struggles in the new country where she arrived with a child but with no money, no marketable skills, or someone to fall back on when needed. She had to start all from scratch. She initially landed in Phoenix, Arizona, and faced the problems head-on: getting a shelter, a job, and a daycare for her boy. She sought support from some acquaintances and the people she met. Despite some kindness from a few individuals, her problems are far from over; she was forced to move to Iowa to be with a relative to face these challenges. Alas, this didn't work out either, and she decided to return to Phoenix again.

The most important aspect of the book narrates how she decided to become an Uber driver to get a stable income for her family after trying many temporary jobs. That was a challenging task too. As a woman Uber driver, she faced many challenges. The new job she embarked on while ensuring her a sustainable income also had many risks. She was involved in traffic accidents, faced racist incidents, and even scary moments with passengers. Her insights and description of changing human behavior, including her clients and friends, are fascinating. Finally, she ended up in Oregon, her third state, where she has now permanently settled and got married, and her son is growing up.

Most importantly, she went back to school to complete her undergraduate studies. She snatched a degree in Public Health pre-medicine and is aspiring for more. After so many years of struggle and hard work, she is now a fulfilled woman and content with what she has achieved without forgetting what she went through. The book's central message is patience and hard work pay, and do not give up on your dream, however tortious the road may be. She concludes: "I got to a good place in life because of my perseverance and persistence. I never stopped moving when life became harsh and difficult". This enjoyable and captivating story is written in a straightforward style, and I recommend it to the members of our community and beyond to learn from the author's shared life story and experiences.

Prof. Abbas Gnamo
Toronto Metropolitan University

AMEN MOHAMMED

Chapter One

The United States: Opportunity and Struggle

I came to the United States of America on September 24th, 2011. I landed in Phoenix, Arizona. I had won the Diversity Visa Lottery in short DV to come to the US. DV is a program the US government gives to individuals from developing countries. My country, Ethiopia, is among those countries. Those individuals can migrate to the US legally and live as permanent residents. I was born to my dad, Mohammed Betera, and my mom, Zeynaba Asfaw, and grew up in a small town called Asasa in Ethiopia. By the way, my name changed from Amane Mohammed Betera to Amen Mohammed when I became a U.S. citizen. I came from a big family, typical of most African families. Mine was very special because my dad has thirty-five children from five wives. He had ten children from my mom—

five girls and five boys. I was a middle child for my mom and a not middle, but a kind of middle for my dad too. Of all those thirty-five siblings, only I came to the US, where I live, to this day. To qualify for the DV program, you must have at least completed the twelfth grade or attended two years of vocational school or an equivalent. The process went smoothly for me because I had already graduated from college and was attending LLB at Law school. On top of that, I was working. I was a journalist.

The online application typically starts in October and ends in November every year. I applied in 2009 on the first week of November. I applied for DV to raise and educate my son in the United States and live a better life. The US was a better place, as many people thought back then. The application system is computerized. The computer randomly selects the lucky individuals who enter the system. Luckily, I was the one that was selected by computer from the 2011 DV entrance to the US. I got accepted around mid-June of 2010. The letter I received stated that as I was a selected candidate, I needed to complete more paperwork for further qualification, and they included information about how to proceed to the next steps. Overall, the process took me a year and a half.

Finally, I came to the US with my three years old son, Obama H Shibo. Imagine migrating with a little boy by yourself. There was excitement about moving to a new country and starting a new life. You know,

OF COURSE, UNDREAMED

America is where everyone wants to live, the place everyone dreams about. Even though I had a good job back home, I wanted to raise my son, Obama, in the US—I even named him Obama after President Baraka Obama!

I was pregnant when Baraka Obama was running for office. I liked his energy and motivational speeches and was especially fond of his motto, "Yes, we can." I was familiar with African American history, and I understand that becoming the president was a remarkable feat for African Americans, considering that there was a time not too long ago when they couldn't even vote. Seeing a Black guy running for president is a miracle, and his father is from the neighboring country Kenya. I kept saying I would name my son Obama if Baraka Obama won the election. Then, Barak Obama won the election, and my son got the name. This was part of why I wanted to bring him to the land of opportunities. I didn't even consider it as taking a risk; I thought it was a better opportunity than my own country.

When I came to the US, I had no close relatives or family I could depend on. My friend asked someone who lived in the US to sponsor me. That person agreed, luckily, because the DV process requires you to have a sponsor. Otherwise, you won't be able to come to the US. The sponsor's job is to help with housing, food, and other necessities until you get settled.

AMEN MOHAMMED

Although I am grateful for those who become sponsors, I am also not happy with them, based on my own experience. Things didn't go the way I imagined. I didn't want to mention my sponsors' names for their privacy, but I weren't happy with how they treated me. They expected me to do whatever they wanted me to do. They always wanted me to be home and didn't like it when I went out.

They didn't want me to communicate with our next-door neighbors—I still do not know why. They didn't want me to get a job. They didn't want me to try anything without their permission. I felt like a little girl who needed approval for anything and everything. There was too much drama, mistreatment, harshness, and backstabbing. They treated me like an unworthy person. They seemed friendly in front of my face, while they talked badly behind my back. They didn't treat my baby as one of their children. The sponsor once called me a bad name, and that's when I started to regret coming to the US. It was so miserable. I didn't imagine it could ever be this bad when I was in my home country. If I had known, I would have stayed in my country.

As a recent immigrant in this new country, I needed to depend on people to start my life from scratch, but my sponsor weren't supportive. On the other hand, I got to know some neighbors while I walked around the apartment building. One day, I begged one neighbor to help me with a job application on their computer because I had left my laptop back home. I applied for a job at the airport in a wheelchair assistance position. Luckily, I got the job but couldn't get to work.

That's when the significant challenges started. Where would I take my son when I went to work? Finding a babysitter and getting a ride to work were my biggest obstacles. I thought I would find a babysitter easily and the government would help me with childcare. I was wrong and discovered that things in Phoenix, Arizona, were problematic. Even public transportation was unreliable, especially in the summer and if you lived far from the city.

On top of that, I didn't even know how to take a bus, and I weren't familiar with the bus route. Everybody had their car. Who was going to show me how to take a bus? I was new to the systems and culture. The people who were meant to help me supposedly were not happy to help me.

So, I needed to figure out how to get around independently. I needed to be smart. I had $250 in my pocket that I had brought from my country. I asked my sponsors if they could get me a phone so I could contact some people to ask for help. They told me I needed to pay for it. I agreed, and as soon as I got a phone number, I started contacting some people I got to know when they came to my sponsor's house to visit. I was 100% confident that my situation weren't comfortable and suitable for me or my son.

I needed to move on. I called one woman whom I got to know through my sponsor. If I recall correctly, my sponsor introduced me to her at the mall. Her name was Tamia. I told her about my situation with fear and mistrust as I was worried; she might tell my sponsor what I told her, and they would retaliate. She expressed her heart to me. And she said she would be happy to help me with anything she could help with.

She said, "I knew your situation before you told me. I don't have your number; thus, I couldn't contact you. Everyone is talking about you. We are all concerned about your sponsor and wonder how they can do this to you, especially with a baby."

I was surprised at Tamia's reaction. She seemed incredibly nice and told me she could even help me with babysitting. I asked her if she could help me with both the baby sittings and give me her extra room, then I could stay with her and pay her for babysitting and room. She didn't want to get in conflict with my sponsors, but at the same time, she tried to help me. She didn't agree to give me a room, but she was happy to help me with Obama. I begged her and cried. Finally, she agreed to let me stay with her. She warned me not to tell anyone I was moving to her house. I assured her that I wouldn't say a word.

This was a miracle for me. I could seek refuge in her house. If it hadn't been for her, I could have ended up on the street, which would have been heartbreaking. At that time, my sponsors had already gotten me a ticket to send me to Iowa. The day I moved was the day I was supposed to fly to Iowa. I called a taxi and left while my sponsor awaited me at the airport. I don't know why they hated to be around me so much—they wanted me to leave the state!

It was in January of 2012 when they wanted me to leave. It was very cold at this point, and I didn't have the proper clothes for myself or my son. As I mentioned earlier, I had no family members to help me. But, thanks to Tamia, I was rescued.

I still feel pain remembering what I had to go through. But let's hold off and talk about something positive instead. I started working as a PSA (Passenger Service Assistance) at Prospect, located inside Sky Harbor Airport, in February 2012. Tamia watched my son when I went to work. I agreed to pay her $400 for babysitting and to rent the room in her home, which weren't big money for her, but it was big money for me. I'm still grateful for her and appreciate her help and kindness.

After I lived with her for two and a half months, I could see her behavior start to shift. She was not the same Tamia who had rescued me. I didn't feel comfortable living with her anymore. Again, I was in another dramatic living situation and felt like I had been taken hostage. I was sick and tired of the drama. As I figured out later, she talked with my sponsors about me when I went to work, and they must have brainwashed her. Whatever the case, I knew I needed to find my place.

While I was at Tamia's house, a man from my country, Jaylan, sold me his old car with a small down payment and agreed to the rest with a monthly fee. I got the car. But I wondered, who was going to teach me how to drive? It was ironic; I had a car but couldn't drive. Thus, I had to find someone who could give me driving lesson. I searched for a driving school and found one Somalians owned. I paid $250 for the class, and the owner assigned someone to teach me how to drive. That guy instructed me for about two hours before saying, "You are ok; you can take the test with us." I was shocked when he said I was ok. I was *not ok,* and I couldn't take the driving test. I knew I would fail if I took the test. I had already taken the five-hour class and received my learner's permit three months prior when I was living at my sponsor's house. Sadly, I needed to hold off on driving school and focus on moving out. I told the guy who sold me a car to find a roommate. The guy asked his friends if they knew someone looking for a roommate. And ultimately, he found me a roommate.

Moving out of Tamia's house was imminent. She had already changed. Her attitude had already changed. Whenever she got upset somewhere or with someone, she blamed me. She took all her anger out on me and my son. She yelled at me and blamed me for everything. She told me she didn't care if I moved out. There is mistreatment, diminishing, and back stubbing that I didn't like, and I'm tired and sick of it. Giving a bad name was becoming common. She even said to me one day,

"Nobody wants you; you are an unworthy person. You passed your difficulty and problem onto me. Your difficulties and problems are like diseases you pass on to others. I don't want to suffer with you. You go find your place and live by yourself." She was so harsh. After a while, she told me too, as she regretted whatever she said and apologized. Still, that was the day I decided to move out. I knew I would be in a terrible situation again with my son, but I preferred maintaining my dignity.

I moved to my apartment with my new roommate. Her name was Tsehay. I thank God for that. Now, I have my room, and I have my personal space. I love my privacy, which I had been deprived of since I arrived in the US. But still, at the same time, I had to deal with my babysitting problem. Tamia was not going to watch my son anymore. She weren't even happy when I moved out. She didn't even say goodbye to me when I left her house. She just went to her bedroom and didn't come out when I called her. I left her there and left her home.

So, who is going to babysit my son now? I applied for government daycare assistance and was on the waiting list. I called them after two weeks to check if they could move me up to the priority waiting list, but they didn't. I went to a couple of private childcare places. They were so expensive, and I couldn't afford that.

When I moved out of Tamia's house, I hoped that DHS would assist me with daycare. And I became so desperate again. What could I do? Nothing, except praying day and night, asking God for his mercy and help. This was a moment in time when I wanted to commit suicide. I tried to contact Tamia to ask for an apology. She ignored me; clearly, she didn't want to talk to me. There was no organized Oromo Ethiopian community in Phoenix to ask for help.

On the other hand, I heard the Somalian community helped their people. One day, I went there to ask if they could help me with my little boy. Someone took me to the office of a community case worker. He started speaking Somali, but I didn't know the language. He must have thought I was Somalian. He said, "If you are Somalian, you should speak your language."

I told him my dad was Somalian and my mom was Ethiopian. I grew up in the capital city of Ethiopia, Addis Ababa, and that's why I don't know Somali. My dad hadn't taught me Somali.

He looked at my face and said, "You are not Somali, don't lie. We don't have any resources for other people except for our community," and added,

OF COURSE, UNDREAMED

"Sorry for the inconvenience, but find your community, then they can help you."

He didn't even give me a minute to express my situation. He left me hopeless, and I left the place crying.

When one door closes on you, God will open another for you. My roommate Tsehay promised that she would watch my son for two days, and after that, I would have a day off. I took five days off to find a babysitter. I'm thankful for Tsehay. She introduced me to two of her friends, our neighbors. They helped us find an apartment, too. Their names were Abdisa and Tade, and they were from Ethiopia, too. Both were charming people. They knew about me and my situation before I even told them. They felt sorry for me and said that being a single mom isn't easy in America. They appreciated my strength and advised me not to give up. Both promised to teach me driving and that they would watch my son when they were at home until I found a babysitter. They knew I had a car, so they took on the responsibility of teaching me how to drive every weekend. Abdisa would teach me one week, and Tade would teach me the other. They switched it off. Whenever one person took me for a driving lesson, the other would watch my son.

Abdisa and Tade rescued me. I owe them a lot. I relied on them for everything: driving, shopping, and getting rides to work. While they taught me to drive and watch my son, Tade told me he knew a woman who babysat in her apartment. He said,

"Currently, she watches her grandchildren. If she does for others than her grandchildren, I will ask her and tell you what she said." Another time, when we went driving, he told me that the lady was happy to babysit my son. I knew that lady before somewhere.

Afterward, I started dropping my son off with her by driving my car with my learner's permit. I took a risk, as always. It is illegal and very dangerous to drive alone with a permit. On top of that, I drive with a permit while a minor is with me. If the cops had stopped me, I would have been in big trouble.

They were confident I could take the driving test after they taught me every weekend for a month. So, I took the test and passed. From that moment forward, I became independent. I had my driver's license. I could go confidently to work, and I could take myself shopping. I didn't have to drive only on backroads to hide from the cops.

The woman whom Tade had introduced me to watch my son for a couple of months. One day, as I was picking him up, she told me that she was not going to babysit my son due to her son was going to Africa for a vacation for two months. She said,

"I need to go to my son's house, which is far from here, and I need to stay there until he returns." When I asked her how soon she would be leaving, she said,

OF COURSE, UNDREAMED

"In two weeks from now." With that, I felt like someone had hit my head with a big hammer. My heart was achy. I felt hopeless, like I was an unworthy person. I thought my suffering with my little one was over, but it weren't. I just bounced from one problem to another. No gap. Challenges and difficulties were becoming my besties.

One evening, while thinking about the difficulties ahead, I asked myself, why can't I call Hawo? Hawo was Tamia's friend, whom I got to know through Tamia. The following day, I called Hawo and told her I wanted to share something.

Hawo replied,

"I was thinking about you, and I swear I had a plan to call you this evening." She added,

"How is everything? Your son, your roommate, and work?"

I told her everything was ok, but I was still struggling.

"I need your help, Hawo. I couldn't find a permanent babysitter. I'm struggling." As I spoke, I wanted to cry, but it was as if something was stuck in my throat. Hawo was at work so she couldn't talk to me much, but she promised to call me back later before she hung up.

She called me right when she got off work. I told her everything. She felt sorry for me and motivated me to keep moving. She said,

"Never give up. Be strong. Everything will change. Your struggle is temporary. You will find relief one day. Just keep praying and keep moving. Afterward, when your son becomes 12 years, you will not suffer that much be strong. Never stop moving."

I was listening to her preaching and used it as a therapy.

She continued, "I have a guest joining me this Saturday at my home. Would you come?"

I said I would.

She replied,

"I will introduce you to one woman who just came from Nairobi, Kenya, as a refuge."

Hawo is the person who helped me move out of Tamia's house. She helped me with driving my car to my new apartment. When I moved, I didn't have anything except two suitcases. Hawo gave me some household goods and cooking utensils for my new apartment. Tamia was angry with her for helping me move out.

I couldn't wait until Saturday to visit Hawo and her friend. I bought some fruit and went to her house early. She had already finished cooking and was the best cook I had ever met. (She owns the Juba restaurant in Mesa, Arizona, close to ASU. If you want to eat and enjoy Mandi, go there. She made the best Mendi! And so delicious!) That day, I just helped her with cleaning. Her guest came after a while, at around noon. We introduced ourselves with Hawo's leading.

I said, "My name is Amane."

She said, "My name is Ashrafi."

We said to each other, "Wolbarumsa gaari" in our language, which means 'nice meeting you.' We spoke Afaan Oromo. A moment later, we started eating. Hawo made us delicious coffee too. When Ashrafi and I were chatting, Hawo would sometimes come in-between conversations and say in Afaan Oromo language,

"Taphadha," which meant that we had to keep chatting. Through our conversation, I learned that Ashrafi was a single mom like me, and she just arrived from Kenya at a refugee camp last week. It was a golden opportunity for me, I realized. She told me her history, and I told her mine, too. We have one thing in common: being a single mom. Finally, she offered to help me with my son. She said she would watch him for me if I dropped him at her apartment until she found a job.

She said, "I am a single mom. I know how it feels, the struggle, the challenge, the hardship, and the difficulty. I feel you, my sister." She touched my shoulder.

I can't tell you how happy I was when she said,

"Don't worry." I hugged her very tightly. We hugged each other. I started crying, but this time, tears of joy.

She said,

"I'll help you today, and you will help me tomorrow. We will help each other." I promised to invite her to my apartment right before I left.

I invited her to my apartment within two days. Since the day I met, we have become like sisters. We shared, and we cared for each other. I kept dropping my son off for a while at her place with no worries. I was still working at the airport as a PSA providing wheelchairs for people who needed wheelchair assistance. It was an excellent job. People tipped me well.

One day, I was assigned an old lady who needed wheelchair assistance to get to her connecting flight. I needed to take her from one terminal to another. While I was pushing her, she asked me where I was from. I told her I was from Ethiopia.
She said,

"I love Ethiopia, and I was there during Ethiopian Millennium." That is the year 2000 in the Ethiopian Calendar. Ethiopia is the only country that has its own calendar. The Ethiopian Calendar is different from the whole world. The Ethiopian calendar is seven years behind the Gregorian calendar. In the year 2000 in Ethiopia, it was 2007 in the Gregorian calendar.

She added,

"I love the food and the culture, and the people are so nice too." I listened to her the whole way to the other terminal, assuring her that what she was saying was true. We had a wonderful conversation. When we finally got to the terminal, I saw she was going to British Colombia, Canada. It was time to say goodbye. Her plane had arrived, and she was about to get on the jetway. Someone was there to take her inside.

But before we parted ways, she said, "Hold on, I have something for you." I couldn't wait to see what she was going to give me. She opened her handbag, took out her wallet, and dipped her two fingers inside to reveal a $100 bill. She said, "Here is your tip." She continued, "This is my gift to you to buy perfume or a good lotion with it. Thus, you will remember me always."

I was so shocked. Nobody had ever given me such a large tip before. I thanked her, appreciated her, and asked her permission to hug her. She agreed, and we hugged.

Then she said,

"You are a very smart young lady. Go back to school, educate yourself, and change your life unless you want to do this your entire life." That was a big gift and valuable advice that she gave me. Nobody had advised me to go back to school.

I wish I had taken her phone number so I could call her and tell her where I am today. Her advice opened my eyes. I made $150 in tips that day. This is how I imagined Americans to be—kind and giving. This was the magic of America.

Since that day, I convinced myself that going to school would be a good idea. I started looking for another job that would be more convenient for my schedule to go to school. After a while, I got a caregiver job at Arizona Mentor. I started working there and registered for a fall class in 2012 at Phoenix Community College. Thanks to my friend Ashrafi, I didn't have to worry about babysitting—at least for the moment. I worked Friday evenings, Saturdays, and Sundays, the whole day. Monday to Friday, in the morning, I dropped my son off with Ashrafi, and then I went to school. This lasted for a couple of months. Then, I found a program called First Things First, where my son could stay for six hours. It was a kind of 'head start' school. Life was finally good, but this didn't last.

One day, I don't know what happened, but when I got to my friend Ashrafi's home, she was in a bad mood. I didn't want to bother her, so I just dropped Obama off and left for work. Until this day, we had been so nice and peaceful to each other. God knows what happened—suddenly, she weren't the Ashrafi I knew and loved. I couldn't see her welcoming face, and I couldn't understand why. She just changed out of nowhere. It was so heartbreaking. Anyway, I dropped my son and left, and I figured I'd ask her what happened when I returned from work later.

When I arrived after work, she weren't home. My son was with her children at home. I asked the kids where she went. They said she went to a grocery store. She doesn't usually go anywhere at my pickup time. This was strange. I suspected that someone might have been twisting her mind or brainwashing her. Maybe someone was questioning why she watched my son for free. I had offered her some money the first time I dropped Obama off, but she refused. I even gave my old Nissan Sentra to her so she could learn how to drive. So, I didn't understand what was happening. I just took my son and left. While I was driving home, I called her, but she didn't answer.

In the morning, I called her to tell her that I was coming to drop off my son.

She literarily said,

"Don't come today. I am not home. Find someone who will watch him." Then, she hung up. I tried calling her multiple times, but she never picked up the phone or called me back. I had a feeling in my gut that something was going on.

I was getting sick of fake people. One day, they're nice, and another day, they're the opposite. I was tired of people's drama. I called off work and stayed with my son. Again, I was experiencing another sudden change. I stopped dropping my son off with her for no reason. She didn't tell me why she stopped watching my son until today.

Chapter Two

Moving to Iowa

I got to know my relative, Rabirra, through my sponsors after I had arrived in the US. He lived in Iowa. Before I moved into Tamia's house, my sponsor wanted to send me to him. Back then, I refused to go to Iowa and instead moved to Tamia's house and stayed in Arizona. I didn't know Rabirra in person. We chatted through Messenger. My great-grandpa and his great-grandpa were cousins. His family lived far from home—which is why we don't know each other and had never met in person. He came to the US, like me, through DV. Once I started to get settled, we began calling each other.

Now, it was the time to ask for his help by sharing my difficulties with him. One day, I called him and told him about my situation and the fact that I didn't have any way to get out of it. I told him I couldn't go to sleep since the day my friend Ashrafi refused to babysit my son. I told him how many things I tried that just weren't working. I told him I was hopeless and stressed out. I told him that sometimes I wanted to do something crazy to myself, and I was struggling with my negative thinking.

Whenever I think about doing something to harm myself, my son's face appears in my mind. As soon as that happens, I regret and repent for thinking bad things. I convince myself that tomorrow will be a better day. I knew that the more I challenged my negative self-talk, the stronger I would become. But how would I pass through this challenging time? I always said, "If I'm not strong and pass this challenge, who is going to teach my son how to be strong?" I needed to live for him. If I died, nobody would be there to care for him, and he will end up in a foster home. I didn't like that kind of life for him. So, I repented right away for my bad thinking.

Rabirra listened the whole time I was talking. I told him I would love to return to Ethiopia, but I didn't have a penny to my name to get a plane ticket. I worked and paid my bills. That's it. I didn't have money. I didn't want to beg people for money. I kept talking to him without stopping. I explained that I applied for SNAP,

and they gave me $100 a month. "Rabirra, you know that isn't enough money, even for food. I am developing depression from too much stress."
When I paused to take a breath, Rabirra interrupted me.

"I do understand life isn't easy even when you are alone, let alone with a little boy." He continued,

"If you want to, you can move in here, and we will help each other. It is better to be close." His offer gave me a little bit of relief. From that day forward, Rabirra called me every other day before he went to work. He told me that it wouldn't be difficult to find a babysitter if I moved to Iowa.

He said,

"Some women do childcare here; you can contact them when you arrive. Meanwhile, don't think and worry too much, please. Take care of yourself. You need to be alive for your son." Just before he hung up the phone, he said,

"Take care of yourself." But I didn't like that word. How could he think that? I was stressed about how I would take care of myself. Instead, it seemed easier to just end my life.

In a rush, I decided to move to Iowa. Ashrafi weren't speaking to me. She was completely ignoring me. I needed to decide to move out before next month's bills came. That meant that I needed to decide within two weeks. It was mid-October of 2013. I knew this decision was so rushed; I just wanted a change. I was a student at PCC, and I needed to drop out of all my classes.

At that time, I was dating someone that I couldn't rely on because of his own difficulty. His name was Esme. Esme had a caring personality. I called Esme and told him to stop by my house after work one afternoon. He came right after work, and I made bread and tea for dinner. After we chatted for a little bit, I told him I wanted to move out. He looked sad and sorry for me. He asked me where I was moving and when I planned to leave. I told him in two weeks.

He said, "That is rushed."

I told him that I had no choice, as Ashrafi was ignoring me, and I didn't have a babysitter.

He asked, "Then where are you moving?"

I replied, "Iowa."

"Why Iowa?" he asked.

I explained that my cousin lived there.

He said, "Ok, that is nice. Sorry, I couldn't help you."

I said, "I know. It is all right."

So, I needed to put all my stuff on sale and give the rest to the people whom I knew. I got rid of all my belongings except my car Nissan, Murano. Esme called me to ask me the exact day I would be moving out. I told him it would be on the 12th of October 2013. He supported my decision to move, but he promised that he would eventually bring me back to Phoenix when he would be financially capable of supporting us. I didn't have a choice but to accept whatever he said. Then, we confirmed the day we would leave. I told Esme as I wanted to take my car with me. We agreed to drive my car all the way to Iowa. After he took us there, he would fly back to Phoenix. I booked him a flight.

It was move-out day, October 12th, 2013, around 5:00 p.m. Esme came directly from work, and my son and I were already ready. We got something to eat and filled up a tank with gas. We hit the road around 5:30 p.m. Esme, Obama, and I was in the Murano. I said bye to Phoenix, hoping to return one day. I weren't very happy leaving Phoenix, but situations forced me to leave, especially the difficulty of finding and keeping a babysitter. I was only moving out to get help.

As we drove east on our first day, headed to the Midwest, Esme was the driver most of the time, while I only drove for about thirty minutes. Esme continued driving until 12:00 a.m. I could see from his face that he was getting tired and needed to take a break. By then, we were in Albuquerque, New Mexico. We needed to find a motel or something like that to rest. What we weren't aware of was the fact that the day we were there was a hot air balloon holiday. There were no rooms available in any hotel or motel in New Mexico. It was a big holiday, and every hotel and motel w fully booked. We drove here and there, but there was no hotel. Finally, we decided to keep driving until we found a motel. I told Esme we could even sleep in our car, but he refused. I could see from his face that he was exhausted. We drove for about an hour, and we found a small town. Then we saw there was a hotel— a Holiday Inn. We stopped and asked the front desk if they had a room.

The front desk lady said,

"Yes, we have one room that has one king bed and one sofa." We were happy to get the room, even if it didn't have enough beds for all three of us. We were tired. My son was sleeping on and off. It was 2:00 a.m. by the time we booked the room. We took our luggage out of the car and went to the room. Esme slept on the sofa. My son and I slept on the king-size bed. I paid around $150. We couldn't wake up in the morning because we were so tired and slept until 11:00 a.m.

In the morning, after we ate breakfast, Esme started driving toward Iowa. We passed Denver, Colorado, and crossed a few small cities in Colorado. We didn't want to drive for long hours like we did the previous day, so we decided to get rest early. Esme stopped driving at around 6:00 p.m. in Nebraska. We found a motel in Lincoln and stayed there for the night.

The next day, after we ate breakfast, we started driving towards Iowa. It's still a blur to me which cities we passed through in Colorado, Nebraska, or even Iowa. After a half day of driving, finally, we arrived in Sioux City at around 1:00 p.m. Rabirra was home when we got there. It was October 14th, 2013, a Sunday afternoon. He welcomed us to his second-floor apartment. The apartment was old; it looked like it had been built in the late eighteenth century. It needed a lot of fixing. The floor was dirty, the wall was scratched, the roof was very dirty and leaked in the bathroom, and the window was cracked. Cold air came through that cracked window. On top of that, it had a lot of pests like cockroaches, rats, and bed bugs. I wanted to take a shower so badly, but the tub was moldy and smelly.

Rabirra brought us some food from outside, but none of us had an appetite. My son saw a rat running around, and he became terrified. Esme went to tour around the city with Rabirra while my son and I stayed in the apartment. They were out for an hour and came back. Obama told Esme that he saw a rat as soon as they returned. Esme weren't surprised about the news of the rat; he had already seen it before us, but he didn't want to say anything. We were all tired and went to sleep. Esme slept on the old and ripped couch, and my son and I slept on the mattress that was on the floor. We needed to get our rest, as Esme had a flight in the morning from Omaha, Nebraska, to go back to Phoenix.

In the morning, Rabirra and his friend took Esme to the airport. They used my car. Esme flew back to Phoenix. When Esme left us, I wept like a baby again. I felt lonely and cried and cried. He promised to bring me back to Arizona when he would finally be financially capable of supporting us. My heart felt broken when he left. My son even started crying. He asked me why he was leaving. He thought Esme would be staying with us. Right then, I promised I would take us back to Phoenix, with or without Esme's help.

In Iowa, everything was sickening and depressing, including the weather, the apartment, and the food. The weather was so cold I could feel it in my bones. The apartment was old and didn't have a good heater, and the window was cracked and let the cold air in. I couldn't find nice restaurants except for a few Somalian restaurants. It was hard to cook in the kitchen in the apartment, too. I didn't have cooking utensils, and Rabirra didn't have any, either. He didn't cook. He always ate with his girlfriend.

I didn't know anyone in Sioux City except Rabirra. After we got there, it seemed like he didn't have a real interest in helping me. He barely communicated with me. He was not the Rabirra I knew on the phone. He weren't supportive. I also got the feeling that his girlfriend was not happy with me moving there. So, I needed to be self-dependent. I need to be strong and resilient in the face of hardship. I already messed so much up; I didn't want to mess up more.

OF COURSE, UNDREAMED

What made things even more difficult was that Rabirra worked five days a week. Saturday and Sunday were his only days off. I couldn't depend on him that much. He did his shopping and laundry on Saturday with his girlfriend. On Sunday, he just spent his time in bed. He didn't like to be bothered. He stayed in bed for half of the day on Sundays. He got irritated easily.

Right away, I started looking for a job; at the same time wanted to take a CNA class. He told me when I was in Phoenix that CNA jobs were plentiful in Iowa. If I took a CNA accelerated course, he said, it would be very easy to get a job. His recommendation was to take a CNA right away when I got to Sioux City. As we talked, I started looking for CNA classes and stopped looking for a job. I found one that started in November. I registered right away before it became full, and I paid the $850 fee with my credit card.

Rabirra weren't happy when I told him about my registration for the CNA class. He was worried about money and bills. It was clear that he wanted me to find my own place or start sharing the cost of rent.
He literarily said,

"You need to pay rent. We will share the bill."

I replied,

"What rent? I thought you were helping us. You have been living here, in this apartment, paying rent just fine before we arrived. What makes things different now? We are just sleeping on the floor in your living room. You didn't tell me when I was in Arizona about sharing the bills. You were living by yourself before we came. Did you rent this apartment because of us? Tell me the truth."

He said,

"I had a roommate before you arrived. When you told me you were coming, I kicked him out."

I said,

"You shouldn't have done that, and you should have told me about the rent, too. I don't have money right now. You need to pay your rent. I will share the bill when I'm done with my CNA class and get a job. Until then, don't ask me for any money. Just pay your rent. I only have some money for food, that's it."

Imagine? I moved out to get help, and now I needed to help someone working five days a week and working overtime. How was I ever going to pay rent without work? I was broken.

He was so mad and crazy. He said,

"You have been in America for two years; how could you not have money? Shame on you!"

That was embarrassing and insulting for me. He didn't understand my situation at all, and I didn't know why he advised me to move out in the first place. Where was that commitment he had promised? I was a single mom, struggling with life by myself in a new and unfamiliar country. How could I have saved money?

Ever since that day, Rabirra and I didn't get along with each other. He was selfish and greedy. He didn't care if we settled or not. He didn't care if I was broken or not.

So, I was ready to start CNA in November.

Meanwhile, Rabirra was curious about what I planned to do with my son when I started taking the class. In the meantime, I was looking for an Ethiopian babysitter. One day, I was at an Ethiopian mini market to get Ethiopian bread, Injera. Someone approached me and asked me if I had just come from Ethiopia because I looked new. Of course, I was new to the area. I told him I came from Phoenix, Arizona. We chatted together for a while, and before we parted ways, he told me not to be a stranger. We exchanged phone numbers. After that, he called me sometimes and checked to see if I was doing well and getting used to the area. As it turned out, he was the person who found me a babysitter, too. He called me one day and gave me the babysitter's phone number. After talking with him, I called her and told her I was new to the area and that I was a single mom looking for childcare. Then, I asked her if she could babysit my son.

She agreed. She was a very nice lady. Then, I asked her how much she would charge per hour.

She said,

"For now, it is ok; you will pay me when you get a job."

I said,

"Are you sure?"

She repeated,

"It's ok; you don't need to pay me anything for now; just bring your son when you need help."

I couldn't believe it. What a blessing this was! Someone I didn't even know extended their hands to help me. I was thankful to her. Life can be so unexpected. Someone you trust can turn their back on you one minute, and then the next, a stranger is willing to help. What a miracle it was! Even when a person you trust betrays you, God has his own plan for you.

When I started the CNA class, I would drop my son at school and pick him up when he was finished. My classes began at 8:15 a.m. and ended at 2:15 p.m. On Saturdays and Sundays, I didn't have a class. I went to in-person classes for four weeks, and I needed to do clinical for the last two weeks before I completed the course and got the license. This was a challenging time for me because the clinical started at six o'clock in the morning. I needed to wake my son at 5:00 a.m., then drop him off at the babysitter, who would then drop him at school in the morning. After school, I could pick him up. I dropped him off with her around 5:30 a.m., then would go to the clinic for two weeks.

OF COURSE, UNDREAMED

Finally, I completed the class and got my CNA license. Right away, the agency that gave us the course wanted us to work for them. I didn't hesitate to accept the offer because I needed to start working and pay Rabirra for the living room where we were staying. The rent is $350. So, I need to pay half of the rent and the electricity bill in full. He told me to pay the electricity bill in full because he didn't cook or use the heater. Apparently, I was the only one who used the electricity for cooking and heat.

He said,

"You are the one who cooks and uses the heater all the time, so you need to pay the bill." He asked me to pay the Wi-Fi bill, but I don't even have a computer. I refused to pay the internet bill, which was thirty-two dollars. That dude really loved money! He was very greedy. He loved money more than anything in the world. He always argued and fought with me about simple and unnecessary things, especially when it came to money. He didn't have any tolerance when it came to me. I didn't want my son to pick up his behavior. Most of the time, I didn't want to be home when he was home. He always liked to find little things and argue about them. That was the reason I chose to work Saturday and Sunday, which were long shifts.

The agency gave me a twelve-hour shift on Saturdays and Sundays, and it was an hour-long drive from my place to a nursing home in Laurel Crest,

Nebraska. I started work at 10:00 a.m. and ended at 10:00 p.m. On top of that, I had to drive an hour to work and an hour back home. On my way back home, I had to drive in the middle of nowhere and in the middle of the night. When I drove, I was always very scared. There were no streetlights on the road; it was just dark. In addition, it was winter, and there was a lot of snow on the ground, too. It was very dangerous, but God protected me, and I did it for two months.

The CNA job didn't work well for my schedule because it didn't work with my son's schedule. I didn't want to take him to the babysitter every day early in the morning or pick him up late in the evening. On top of that, he weren't happy with staying at the babysitter's house. At the same time, two days' work weren't enough for me to cover my bills and pay Rabirra's rent. I couldn't do CNA because the shift started at 6:00 a.m., 2:00 p.m., or overnight shifts, which began at 10:00 p.m. That weren't convenient for me.

On top of that, I was tired of driving in the jungle in the middle of the night, and I didn't want to do it every day. So, I needed to find another job. I needed to find a job where I could start around 8:00 a.m. and get off before three o'clock in the afternoon. Finally, I found a job at Big Kmart. It was a cashier position, and it was part-time. Perfect, that's what I was looking for. It was a big relief, aside from the fact that one day a week, I started work at 7:00 a.m. That was the only day that I needed to drop Obama off with the babysitter. Other than that, it was a good situation.

One day, on a Monday, my son didn't have school. I needed to go to work at 8:00 a.m. He was sleeping. I tried to wake him up, but he was so tired that he couldn't. Rabirra was home, so I asked if he could drop Obama at the babysitter's house when he left for work.
I said,

"Rabirra, Obama isn't getting up for now. I am late for work. Can you please drop him at the babysitter's house when you go to work? Please!"

He agreed, and I trusted him and left for work.

At around 2:45 p.m., I felt a butterfly in my stomach. I felt a kind of stomach ache. So, I had to ask my boss to go to the restroom for five minutes. I could tell that something was just not ok. My boss gave me five minutes. I went to the restroom, and while I sat on the toilet, I took out my phone and checked to see if I had a missed call. As it turned out, my gut instinct was correct, and Rabirra had called me many times. My body started shaking. He left me a voicemail. I was scared to listen to it. I was afraid to hear something bad about my son. Without a choice, I listened to it.

"Amane, I left Obama at home; he doesn't want to go to the babysitter's house, so don't stay at work late. He is home by himself."

I became numb. I felt nauseous, and I wanted to vomit. My body started shaking. I didn't know what to do. My son couldn't stay by himself at home. Rabirra left him at 1:45 p.m. Obama had already been alone for an hour. He didn't have a phone; thus, I couldn't call him and check on him or warn him not to go outside.

I didn't even know if he was home or if he ran away because of the rat. After all, he was extremely scared of that rat. Obama is five years old currently. I cursed Rabirra and my life. In America, you don't leave minors by themselves. Rabirra knew that. How could he do that to me? Was he just trying to hurt me, or had my son truly refused to go? If that was the case, he could have forced or convinced him to go to the babysitter. I needed to rush. I needed to tell my boss that my son was in danger. Half of me was dead. I needed to go home immediately.

I told my boss my son was sick.

What happened?" she asked.

I said, "I don't know."

Then, she said, "Ok, just go."

It was in January. It was very bad weather. It was snowy and slippery. Imagine my situation! I didn't have much experience driving in the snow. Usually, I just drove very slowly and carefully. Now, I need to drive fast. There was some ice on the ground, and the road was slippery, too. I didn't care about all that; I just wanted to see my son. At the same time, I wished Rabirra was home, too. I wished Rabirra didn't leave Obama at home by himself.

In my imagination, I saw something happening. My son really didn't like rats, and if he were to see a rat, he would scream and run away. Maybe that's what happened, I thought. Then people would see him and report me for abandoning him. Or someone could steal him from the apartment. Still, I drove my car, sliding from side to side. When I stopped at the traffic light, the wheels spun. While I was driving, I called my babysitter and told her to rush to the apartment. I told her that Rabirra left him alone.

I told Rabirra to drop him at your house when he leaves, but he left him home. Please go there. I was crying. She didn't have a car. She needed to walk. Still, I was driving like crazy, sliding everywhere. I was lucky there was not much traffic other than a few cars on the road.

Finally, my babysitter and I arrived at the same time. She grabbed the key from me and ran all the way to the second floor. I couldn't leave the car. I didn't want to face the truth if my son was not home. I just fainted for a while. My heart was pounding. I could even hear my heartbeat in my ears. While I struggled to come out of the car, she came back to me and said,

"He is home; he is home; he is fine." She continued,

"He is home, watching TV."

I tried to catch my breath. It took me fifteen minutes to come to my mind. I hated my life again. I hated Rabirra. Was this revenge? Why would he do this to me? I wouldn't say I liked Iowa again. In general, I hated everything. I could've died of a heart attack or panic attack. I cursed Rabirra more and more!

When I got home, I was scared to look at my son's face as if I had done something bad to him. I felt guilty. I thought I'd lost him for a second. I thought I brought him to Iowa for a better life, not for a worse life. Finally, my babysitter, Hasna, calmed me down, took me to her house, and made me food and coffee. She was a nice lady. She advised me not to panic, or I could die of a heart attack, or something bad could happen to me. And she told me not to worry too much.
She said,

"Just leave all your worries and your son to your God; he is not going to betray you; believe in Him." That is the kind of preaching I needed at that moment. She promised me again that she would continue to help me and be there for me any time. I thanked her profusely.

Working in Kmart weren't bad except for some people asking me why I covered my head, which irritated me a lot and became annoying when they asked me this question frequently. Some people thought the reason I covered my head was because I was too cold. It was obvious the weather in Iowa was too cold for me. I was used to Phoenix, Arizona, the desert of the US, where it never got cold. But the reason I covered my head weren't only because of the weather—it was my culture and my identity, too. What I experienced in Iowa was that people liked to generalize and make assumptions.

The CNA job itself weren't always fun, either. The nurses sent me home sometimes without sufficient reason. I remember two days that I was sent home for no reason. One time, I was assigned to an old lady who liked only one person. Every time I entered her room, she kept asking me where that person was. I tried to tell her the person was somewhere else, helping other seniors, and he would be back soon. She weren't happy when I tried to help her, and she refused whenever I offered to help her. She keeps saying,

"Bryan knows how to do this and that." It was so annoying, but I was very patient with her and kept helping her until she started yelling at me for no reason when I was helping with putting on her wristband. I told the nurse in charge about the situation, but the nurse didn't say anything and kept sending me there when her call light was on. I already told her not to send me there and asked her to switch me with someone. It was clear that the lady didn't like me. She kept saying, "Bryan" and "Bryan." The nurse refused my request and sent me home.

Another time, there was another old lady who knew a little bit about Ethiopia. Specifically, she knew about the famine that happened in 1972. She asked me right away where I was from. I told her I was from Ethiopia.
She said,

"Um, that famine I remember, is it still going on right now?" She assumed that Ethiopia was still in famine. She added,

"Ethiopia is a poor country. Isn't it? Do you have enough to eat there?"

I replied,

"Yes, ma'am, we have plenty of food right now, and we are even exporting some foods to different countries, including the US."

She continued,

"Why did you come here if you have enough to eat at home and have extra food to export? I thought you guys were running away from famine and a corrupt government."

She made me angry. I ignored her for a moment. The question she was asking was deliberate, and she was only asking to make me mad. Whenever I passed by her, she always said something inappropriate. She put me in such an uncomfortable position I could barely bring myself to help her. I tried to stay away

from her as much as I could, but she kept throwing mean words at me. When I was adjusting the table at lunchtime, she called me and yelled,
"Hey, you, what is for lunch?"

I said,

"I don't know. I will ask the kitchen people for you. Didn't they bring you the menu to choose what you want for lunch? Anyway, I will ask for you."

And then, without reason, she said,

"I know why you are an idiot.

I was so mad when she called me an idiot. I reported it to the nurse, but she sent me home. When I think about it today, it's clear that it was racism. Both the nurses and the two old ladies were racist toward me. I didn't even ask why they sent me home. I was scared they might retaliate against me. I just accepted and went home. I took it as a relief.

I didn't have that much experience with racism when I was in Phoenix, except one day, I was at Walmart with my son looking for something on the shelf, and one guy who had a gun in his pocket approached me and said,
"You're a terrorist, leave my country and go back to your home." I was shocked, so I immediately grabbed my son's hand and left the store. Except for that incident, I didn't experience racism in Phoenix.

That's another reason that made me decide to go back to Phoenix, even if there's no progress when it comes to Esme's ability to provide. I didn't want to stay in the racist environment of Iowa. I said to myself,
"I don't care what will happen in Arizona. Now I have a CNA license and experience. If I moved back, I would get a job easily. I will be independent. I don't need to depend on anyone financially. Even if I don't get the CNA job right away, I can go back to my old job—a caregiver at Az-mentor."

When I left Phoenix, I didn't say goodbye to anyone except my friend Natsenet and Hawo. Natsenet and I had known each other from back home when we were in law school. Hawo was the friend I had made through Tamia. I still communicated with them regularly, and I told both that I might move back to Phoenix because the situation in Iowa was still horrible.

One day, Natsenet and her husband Zeru called me, and we were talking. My son heard us talking. He liked Zaru. He came close and leaned on me, listening in on my conversation.
When we were done, my son said,

"I want to talk to Zeru."

So, I gave him the phone.

 Zeru said,

"Hello, Obama; how are you doing?"

OF COURSE, UNDREAMED

Obama replied,

"I am not doing good. I don't know where my mom took me. I am not in America. This is not America."

I knew Sioux City didn't look like America—it's a small and old city. I was sorry and sad that my little one didn't feel like he was in America.

Then, to me, Zaru said,

"Bring him back to Phoenix, please. Don't torture him over there." Zaru gave the phone to their son, Jussie who is my son's friend. Jussie and Obama talked to each other for a little bit, then hung up. They used to go to the park and play together. That was the third reason I moved out of Sioux City.

From that day, I started looking for a flight to go back to Phoenix. I hated living in Iowa. Why would I stay there if all my scarifies weren't making my son happy? I wanted to leave. In addition, Rabirra and I had become enemies. I hadn't talked to him since the day he left my son by himself at home. He had a girlfriend, and most of the time, he just spent most of his time in her apartment. He ate there and livcd there. Occasionally, he would come home and lay in bed in his apartment.

Before I bought the ticket, I needed to talk to Natsenet and check if she would let me stay with her until I found my place.

She said,

"Yes, you can stay with us."

I was so happy when she said yes. After that, I got a plane ticket to Phoenix, scheduled to depart on February 20th, 2014. I told Hawo I was moving back to Phoenix. She assured me she would help me as much as she could. So, I then had two assurances. If Natsenet changed her mind, I had a Plan B: Hawo. I hadn't gotten any assurance from Esme.

I shipped my car ahead of time. I loved my car and didn't want to get rid of it. Other than my car, I didn't have that many belongings in Sioux City. It is so easy to move out. I didn't tell Rabirra I was returning to Phoenix until the day before I left. My flight was on Saturday morning. I knew he didn't work on Saturday. I arranged for a taxi to take me to the airport. I told him Friday morning before he went to work that I would be leaving Iowa.

I said,

"Rabirra, I'm flying out tomorrow to Phoenix." He was mad. He thought I was stuck in Sioux City and never going to be able to go back to Phoenix.

He said,

"So, why are you telling me now?"

I said,

"I know that even if I told you ahead of time, it doesn't matter to you. I know you don't care if I move out or not. At the same time, you might be happy because you will get back to your apartment and your roommate. But I don't want to ignore you and leave without telling you. That isn't nice. The reason I'm telling you is to get just peace of mind."

He said,

"I don't care."

I said,

"Whatever!"

He said,

"Who is going to take you to the airport?"

I said,

"Don't worry about it; I already arranged the taxi."

He replied,

"Whatever," adding, "I know you are crazy."

I didn't talk back to him and instead chose to ignore him. He left for work. During the day, I packed our clothes up, and we got ourselves ready for the early morning flight. I went to my babysitter's house to say goodbye. She was sorry to miss us and wished us good luck. I came back from her house in the evening. We needed to sleep early because we had to get up at 3:00 a.m. for our 5:15 flight. I told my son we were going back to Phoenix tomorrow. He was so happy and excited; he couldn't sleep the whole night. We woke up at 3:00 a.m., took our luggage, and got ready for the taxi to pick us up.

Rabirra woke up and said,

"I will take you to the airport," I told him that I already called a taxi, and it was on its way. He insisted and took us to the airport. I canceled the cab. Sioux City Airport is very small, only operating morning flights and small planes. We said goodbye to him and went inside the airport. Right away, our plane came, and we boarded. When we took off, we said "bye, bye" to Sioux City, Iowa.

Chapter Three

Back to Phoenix, Arizona

Our flight had three connecting flights. The first one was to Omaha, the second to Denver, and the final flight was from Denver to Phoenix. We arrived at Sky Harbor Airport around 4:30 p.m. I could feel the warm air and bright sky even before we landed. The warm weather and the clear sky replenished my soul.

Esme was waiting for us at the TSA checkpoint. Obama saw him from a distance and started running toward him. When he reached him, he jumped on Esme, who picked him up and kissed him on his cheeks. They both missed each other.

Then it was my turn. I couldn't wait to hug him, breathe through his neck that burning air from my chest, and let my anger and emotions escape. I was about to cry but forced myself not to. The emotion choked my throat. We hugged each other, and Esme kissed me on my cheeks. I said,

"Finally, I'm here, thank God." Then we picked up our luggage from the carousel and headed to the car. Natsenet was waiting for us, and we all headed to her apartment.

Natsenet's apartment was a ten-minute drive from the airport. As we arrived at her place, she welcomed us. She was the one whom I shared my idea of moving to Iowa with, and again, she was the person whom I talked about coming back to Phoenix. When we arrived, Natsi and Zaru, her husband, welcomed us. Moments later, she gave us some clean towels to shower with before we ate dinner. I gave a shower to my son first then I took a long nice warm shower. I let the warm water run on my head and shoulder for a while. It felt good. It was a kind of healing and relief. I never enjoyed Iowa's water; it was always either too cold or too hot. Even the weather was so different. Then, it was still snowing in Iowa, but Arizona was warm, with the temperature in the mid-seventies. Natsi made us delicious food and coffee.

Making coffee for someone in our culture is so special. You don't just get Kroger or Colombia coffee and make it in a coffee maker. You need to roast and grind the coffee beans, then make them in a special pot called JABANA. The aroma of roasted beans heals your emotion and soul and makes you calm down and relax. Even the coffee cups are different in shape and size. They are called SINI. They have a white stripe with the Ethiopian flag and might hold only a quarter of a cup. The cups sit on a wood, mica, or glass device called RAKABOT. You can get RAKABOT in two shapes—circular or rectangular. It is a kind of ritual ceremony. Every single coffee material, including coffee beans, comes from Ethiopia.

Making coffee for a guest shows your guest how very important they are. It shows the respect your host has for you. At this moment, I felt safety in familiarity. When I moved to Iowa, Rabirra didn't make our coffee. Now that I am back in Arizona, I ate delicious food and drank special coffee. I was thankful for her and Zaru's reception. Most importantly, I thanked them for welcoming me and giving me a place to stay until I found my own place.

I stayed with them for about a month and a half. I enjoyed the time with her, but at the same time, I didn't want to be a burden. So, I needed to find my place. Natsi lived in a three-bedroom apartment and had two children, too. So, I needed to give her a space. I already started looking for jobs in CAN and the caregiver industry.

The problem was that my CNA license from Iowa didn't work in Arizona. I needed to relicense it in Arizona. Every state has its own rules and regulations. Arizona Board of Nursing had to give me a license; otherwise, I couldn't work as a CNA. This process would take a while, so while I waited for the license, I returned to my old job as a caregiver at Az-Mentor. I couldn't return to my old house—someone already took it, so I needed to go to a different house. I chose the night shift because my son sleeps when I go to work, so he doesn't need a babysitter, especially while I am staying at Natsenet's house. I told her about my schedule, and she agreed on that, too. Az-Mentor gave me three-night shifts. Friday night, Saturday night, and Sunday night.

Arizona Broad of Nursing finally gave me my CNA license, but finding a job was so hard, especially with my difficult schedule. There were no flexible shifts. 6:00 a.m. to 2:00 p.m., 2:00 p.m. to 10:00 p.m., or 10:00 p.m. to 6:00 a.m. None of the shifts worked for me. Thus, I held onto my license. If I accept those shifts, my son will be in school, so I need someone to drop him off or pick him up from school. Natsenet works at night, and she sleeps in the morning. If I accept the 6:00 a.m. shift, who will drop him off for me and if I accept the 2:00 p.m. shifts, who will pick him up for me from school? It doesn't work.

After staying with Natsenet for a month and a half, I moved to my place, which was in the same complex but in a different building. My son still stayed with her after I moved to my apartment. They helped me a lot, especially Zaru. He was an extraordinary person. He was the person who took care of my son most of the time. I appreciated him, and I owed him a lot. He was a father figure for my son. He took my son with them whenever he took his son. He was very kind, understanding, and humble.

I continued to drop off my son with them every Friday, Saturday, and Sunday night. But sometimes, when they had their plans, something happened, or there was an event, I would call off work. Other than that, I was 100% happy with my decision to move out of Iowa. For the sake of having a backup plan or for an emergency, I had already approached someone I could rely on.

I was thankful to Natsent and Zaru for everything they had done for me, but sometimes Natsenet complained about my son fighting with her son. Obama was very active; he liked to play and jump around. Other than that, he weren't that bad of a kid. On the other hand, her son didn't like playing too much. Natsenet told me that both boys wrestled many times, and my son would always go hard on her son, which weren't safe for either of them. So, I needed to discipline my son. Every night when I dropped him off, I always said to him, "Baba, you know there is no wrestling. Don't wrestle or play hard."

Despite that, life was ok, but I was still a little bit uncomfortable and lagging with my bills. Natsenet helped me babysit Obama until October 2014. She never asked me to pay her. I'm thankful for her.

Finally, one of my friends, Ashu, who was an athlete, came from Ethiopia to deliver her baby in the

US. She stayed with me for more than half of her pregnancy. I think she came before her second trimester. I was happy to help her, but it was also a big relief for me, too. While she stayed with me, I didn't have to worry about having a babysitter. Ashu came in the middle of October 2014. This was a golden opportunity for me. And, because I didn't have to worry about my son, I could work two or three jobs. Ashu walked Obama to school and picked him up if I weren't home. Obama and Ashu stayed together when I went to my weekend night shift. I helped her with doctor's appointments and follow-ups and gave her a room to sleep in. She didn't need to pay for rent or food. She lived with us and ate with us free of charge. We treated each other like family.

It was December 17th, 2014. While I was at work, one person came with the mail delivery. As Ashu told me, he knocked on the door and asked her to sign the mail receipt. She didn't know what it was. She signed and took the mail from the guy. When I got home, she said,

"One guy gave me this envelope, and he asked me to sign, and I signed for him, and he handed me the mail." I couldn't wait to see what it was. I weren't expecting any mail from anyone. Then, after she handed it to me, I opened it and saw a check and a note inside the envelope. I couldn't believe it. I said,

"Oh my God, who is sending me a check?" I didn't know who would send me a check or why they would send me a check. I kissed the check because it was free money and came at the right time when I was looking for extra cash. I put it next to me on the table and started reading the note. It said as follows:

"You are randomly selected to do secret shopping. We will pay you a commission. Now, deposit this check right away. After you deposit it, get a money order from the deposited check for another secret shopper like you. Do this as soon as possible, and don't wait until the check gets cleared."

The check was made out for 2,500.00 dollars. I was so happy and confused to have this money in my possession.

Right away, I went to Chase Bank and deposited the check.

In the note, it said,

"After you have deposited the check, let us know via the email provided below." Their email address was written in the note. I just did what they said. Then they emailed me back right away to tell me to send a money order to another secret shopper. They told me to make two money orders, one for $800 and one for $1,000, and then send it to the address provided in the note through an overnight mail delivery service. Then, the rest of the money would be mine. Seven-hundred dollars would be mine. I was so happy because I needed extra cash to send to my mom, who was back home. This was a golden opportunity.

I said,

"My mom's prayers were accepted. I started getting free money without working hard. On top of that, they told me not to write any name on the money order. So, I took out the money order in the morning as they requested.

After I sent the money order to their provided address, I emailed them. Then, they responded immediately and told me to go to Walmart and do secret shopping. They told me to take $250 from the rest of the money and do the shopping for myself. They told me to evaluate the cashier about their customer service. They told me to look around and examine how the store was organized, if the shelves were empty or not, and to see if the merchandise was in the right place or if it was easy to find. I bought many things for $250. Finally, they told me to write a report about my shopping experience. I did exactly as they asked and sent my evaluation via email.

After three days, I couldn't sign into my bank account to check the balance. I was so frustrated; I just started my car and ran to the bank. I was shaking. I ran to the teller and asked her why I couldn't access my account. She asked me for my ID and my debit card. I handed it over to her. She looked at my account and said,

OF COURSE, UNDREAMED

"This account is temporarily deactivated due to fraudulent activities. For more information, you can talk to the fraud department.

She told me to be seated and wait for someone to come and talk to me. I about lost my mind. I weren't sure what happened.

Someone came right away and told me what happened. The check I had deposited was a forged check. And I over-drafted around $2000 because I didn't have that much money in my account. So, they suspect fraudulent activities. I started crying in front of him. I told him I was innocent and hadn't done any fraudulent activities. I told him the check was coming from somewhere. He was sorry for me and told me he couldn't help me with anything. And he told me if I didn't pay the over-drafted money back within fifteen days, the bank would sue me. That news was extremely scary. I had lost my money, and I was about to lose myself. The guy left me right there and went inside. I sat there for a while without any solutions. In the end, I decided to go to the police and report the matter.

Meanwhile, I tried to contact those people who sent me the forged check via email, but they didn't answer. I emailed them so many times, but I was met with no response. Before this, they had responded right away. I went to the police station to report the scam, but they told me they couldn't help me because I was involved in fraudulent activities. I left the police station helpless and hopeless. I didn't have a bank account, and I didn't have any money to pay my rent. I left empty-handed.

Luckily enough, Ashu had some emergency money on hand. She gave me that money, and I paid my bill. I paid the bank back their money by working sixteen hours a day. America not only treated me with the difficulty of babysitting but also treated me with scammers.

Ashu delivered her baby on March 23rd, 2015. She delivered the baby through C-section, and I was the one who got to hold the baby right when she was born. I was with her at the hospital for three days until her recovery. During that time, Obama stayed at Natsenet's house. I would go there in the morning to pick him up and drop him off at school, and then I would return to the hospital. Then, after school, I picked him up, fed him, then dropped him back at Natsenet's house. Those three days were exhausting. After we got home, it was wonderful to have a new baby around, but at the same time, it was scary how much the baby cried. But, after a little while, we grew accustomed to the baby.

Ashu stayed with us until July 2015. Unfortunately, it was time for Ashu to go back to Ethiopia. Her husband and her family missed her and the baby. Her flight was on July 19th, 2015. We shopped for the baby and Ashu. We packed all her clothes and baby stuff. I needed to take her to the airport in the morning. Ashu was so excited to go back home. I dropped her at the airport. When I got home, the apartment felt empty; no baby was crying, I felt lonely, and the situation was so depressing. It was so quiet and scary. I started crying, and Obama did, too. Now, it was only Obama and me, as usual. It was a nightmare—a terrifying situation.

I'd been talking to Natsenet about Ashu going back home. I even asked her again if I could drop Obama with her until I found someone to watch him. I hadn't gotten a response from her, and I was waiting patiently. I needed to beg people again for babysitting. I knew Natsent weren't 100% happy to keep Obama during the nights, but I couldn't find someone right away. I stopped working my second job right away when Ashu left. Ever since Ashu left us, things have been getting tough. I became lonely and hopeless.

I couldn't think of anyone I could beg to help me besides Natsenet. Changing my shift weren't even going to help me. I even looked for childcare ahead of time before Ashu left, but I came out empty-handed. I needed to return to Natsenet and ask her what was happening. One day, I went to her apartment and started crying in front of her like a baby. I was sobbing in front of her.

She felt sorry for me and said,

"Amane, you know this is a big responsibility that I'm doing for you, and I must always tell Obama not to jump around and wrestle. Obama is so hyper. He doesn't sit in one place. He jumps around, and he doesn't listen."

When she said all these things, something struck my stomach.

She continued,

"For right now, you can bring him, but sometime soon, you need to find childcare."

I wished she wouldn't say such things about my son. But still, it was a relief that she would watch him. At least I had assurance from her for now. I promised Natsent to find childcare soon. I kept looking and asking people. There were plenty of childcare providers, but my problem was money. I couldn't afford any of the childcare options. They asked for $450 to $500 a month. I could barely cover my bills as it was. Not only that, but their working hours also didn't align with mine.

I was baffled. The government childcare assistance weren't giving me any help. They just put me on the waiting list. So, I started dropping him off again with Natsenet for those three weekend nights, and I continued dropping him off until one day, when I went to their house, they didn't open the door when I rang the doorbell. I rang the doorbell many times, but no one opened the door. Then I called them, but they didn't pick up the phone, and I texted both Natsenet and Zaru, but they didn't text back. I was already late for work, and I was in a panic. I kept calling them, but there was no answer. I hated that day. What could I do? Unfortunately, I had to call off and let the staff know I could not go to work due to a babysitting problem. I know calling out of work at the last minute isn't ok. As usual, I thought they would be home at my drop-off time, and everything would be ok. But I was wrong. Lastly, I called my boss and told her I couldn't go to work due to the problem I had with childcare.

Luckily, my boss understood my situation and took me off the shift. She advised me to call out two hours early if I had a problem. She was right—that is the company rule. I told her the people I relied on hadn't informed me that they would not be home for the night. I was even starting to worry about them. They weren't usually like this. I didn't know what happened to them. They weren't answering the phone. I said,

"This isn't normal. They usually let me know ahead of time if they have something or a program. Today is different." In any case, I got excused from my boss, and I stayed home with my son.

Finally, Natsenet called me around 11:00 p.m. and told me I could drop Obama off. Imagine? I was supposed to start work at 8:00 p.m. How could I get three hours late? She told me they weren't home because they were at the movie theater. I was so mad and asked her why she didn't tell me ahead of time.

I said,

"Natsi, I depend on you; you know today is my workday, and I start work at 8:00 p.m." My voice was getting louder, and I wanted to scream at her, but I couldn't.

She weren't serious, and she said,

"Ohh, I forgot."

I'm sure it was deliberate. She even didn't say sorry. It was like a joke to her.

She said again,

"You can bring him now."

Bro, it is too late now. I said,

"That is fine," and she hung up.

It was Sunday night, which was like my Friday. I didn't have work until next Friday and didn't have to drop him off. But I weren't happy with the way she talked to me. Thus, I wanted to go to her house and talk to her in the morning.

But I didn't go to her house in the morning because I wanted to give her time and didn't want to rush our conversation. I will wait until Thursday. I called her on Thursday afternoon and asked her if she was home.

She said, "I am home."

I told her I wanted to come over.

OF COURSE, UNDREAMED

She said,

"OK," I went there right away and chatted briefly with her. I expressed my feelings when they ignored me last Sunday.

I said,

"You know what, Natsi? I felt like you guys were abandoning me."

She replied,

"Sorry you feel that way, but we decided at the last minute to go to the movie theater." The *Captain America* movie had just come out that weekend. In our communication, I sensed something fishy. Something weren't right. It seemed like she was tired of me.

She continued,

"I want to tell you something, but I don't want to make you feel bad and make your life harder." She continued,

"It is very difficult to decide this, but I'm sorry— we will not keep Obama over the weekends. It is tough for us, especially on Sunday mornings, because your son doesn't want to attend church with us. We can't leave him alone, and we can't force him too to go with us."

When I heard that, I became dizzy and was quiet for a while. I couldn't form any words in my mouth. I hated life again. I asked God why my life always turned out like this. I wondered why He always tested me and my only baby. At the same time, I felt my future would be bright. I knew one verse from the holy book. After many struggles, there will be a relief, a big relief. Just stay patient. When I came across those hard times, I referred to that verse.

After a long silence, I said,

"Never mind, I already suspected something the day you ignored my call." Then, as if she had something for me, I asked her, "What is my solution?"

She said,

"I don't know, my dear, and it is hard for all of us. Please don't take it as a bad thing. We love Obama." She tried to be gentle and added, "I might help you one day a week. Other than that, I can't, my dear."

Again, I started crying like a baby in front of her. I wished I had the power to change things. Natsi was severe now. I needed to think about what I had to do. One thing I didn't know about was the possibility of seeking shelter. Nobody told me about it. I came up with the idea of changing my shift to a day shift. But then, who would pick him up after school? That wouldn't work, either. I must work either from 6:00 a.m. to 2:00 p.m. or 2:00 p.m. to 10:00 p.m. on weekdays. It just wouldn't work with my schedule. I contacted one of my friends and explained my situation to her.

OF COURSE, UNDREAMED

Thankfully, she was willing to help me with one night, temporarily—Saturday night. Natsenet still promised to help me on Friday nights. I was almost there; I just needed someone to help me for one night. Working only two nights a week wouldn't be enough to pay all my bills. Still, I agreed, as I couldn't find anyone else, so I needed to take him with me to work one night a week. I decided right away on the idea of taking him to work. I took him to work every Sunday night. I made him sleep in the car.

I had a nice co-worker, a white guy named Craig. I explained my situation to him, and he was happy to help me. And help me, he did, especially Monday morning. He let me go home early to get my son ready for school. I did this for a couple of months without my boss knowing.

According to our company's rules, no minors are allowed to work. I broke the rule. I took the risk. But the only thing I feared was being on the street and failing. My son slept in the car while I showed my face to clients and coworkers, who left shortly after I arrived. I parked my car in front of the group home so I could hear my son's voice if he said something. Everybody said,

"Don't Park in Amane's spot," but they didn't know why. I would spend the night going back and forth from the car to the house—it was good that our clients slept the whole night without waking up. Another good thing was Arizona's warm weather.

I took my son to work for a while until my boss busted me one night. She was nice but told me what I was doing weren't acceptable. She said bringing my son to work can hurt me and even my son.

She explained,

"I do understand your situation, and I wish I could help you, but unfortunately, I can't. Please try to find childcare or change your shift."

I apologized for breaking the rule. And I promised her I wouldn't do it again. Luckily, she didn't write me up. This was an ample warning, though. I urgently needed to find childcare.

One day, while wandering around the neighborhood, I came up with the idea of going to the Mosque. So, I took a shower and left for Mosque on a Friday. On Fridays, many people come to the Mosque to pray together. After the prayer, everyone greets each other. After I greeted everyone, I greeted one lady who was a very nice-looking lady; her name is Asha. She spoke to me in Somali, but I told her as I didn't speak Somali. Some people have said I look like a Somalian, but I don't. I think that is why some people say,

"Eska worran or mafii ante hay?" That means, "How are you?" In any case, I don't know how, but I saw something nice in her face. She spoke a little English, but we managed to understand each other. Everybody left except her and me—we were the only people at the Mosque. I told her I missed my mom to initiate the conversation.

She said, "Sorry."

I said, "It's ok."

Then, she asked who I lived with. I told her that I lived by myself with my son. She asked,

"Single mom?" and I nodded.

To that, she said,

"Sorry,"

I said,

"What can I do?" Then my tears started flowing down my cheeks.

She looked sad and said,

"What is a problem?"

I told her I was struggling with my son's childcare and was in a very difficult situation. I told her everything about what I was going through.

She felt sad. Then, she said,

"Don't worry, bring your son when you go to work. I don't have work. I will watch him for you."

I told her I worked the night shift.

She said,

"It is okay; that's even better. He goes to sleep while you are gone. It won't bother me."

I offered her a little money for her help. She refused it.

She said,

"Don't worry about it."

I started dropping him off on Friday, Saturday, and Sunday nights. I needed to tell Natsenet and my other friends who kept him Saturday night that I found someone who does childcare. I thanked them for their help, especially Natsenet. Thank God I didn't have to worry that much or take Obama to work with me. And now, I weren't going to have to listen to complaints about my son. She made him breakfast in the morning before I picked him up and even shared some food with me when I arrived. In a way, I felt like I had my mom with me, taking care of me and my son. Life started to get better after I found her. I continued dropping him off with her for a while.

Chapter Four

Uber and Its Experiences

On October 31st, 2015, on Halloween day, I planned to start driving Uber. Before that, I needed to complete an application and requirements. To go for Uber, you need to drive a car that is at most ten years old, have a background check, and have a valid driver's license. I had a 2007 Nissan Murano, my background check was clear, and I had a valid driver's license. That meant I could start driving at any time.

I went to the Uber Hub in Phoenix. It was October 30th, 2015. The process was completed on the same day. Before I started driving, I needed to take the city driving test and score eighty percent or more. I took the test right away, and I passed. The next day, October 31st, 2015, I was ready to be on the road. My Ethiopian friends always talked about Uber. Every conversation was about Uber and how easy it was to make extra money. It was a lucrative job. In every discussion with Ethiopians, Uber was the main topic.

They said,

"You will make money easily, especially if you drive at night, on the weekends, and on the holidays." That is why I decided to drive Uber until it became my primary source of income. Then, I told myself I should start driving on Halloween day. Isn't that funny?

I cleaned my Nissan Murano, filled up gas, and equipped my car with necessities like water and gum for riders. I'd heard that if you offered water and gum to the riders, you would get a five-star rating. I also got a snack for the night, too. I took a long nap to stay up the whole night and be energized. Honestly, I was so excited and eager to be on the road. I was ready to start the night. I arranged the babysitter for my son Obama while I was gone, and then I called one of my friends to ask for his advice and when and where to start. He recommended starting around 8:00 p.m. in downtown Phoenix or Scottsdale. They were known to be good areas to make good money. I got online right at 8:00 p.m. I lived close to downtown Phoenix. A few minutes after I logged on, I got the first-ever request. I started driving towards the pick-up location. I needed to depend on the GPS to find the rider exactly where they were. The first pickup weren't bad because I knew the downtown Phoenix area very well. I rode to the Chandler area and dropped my first rider at the bar. Right away, Uber gave me another ride. That one weren't bad, either.

On Halloween, people dress crazily. The costumes made it hard to differentiate people from one another. My next ride was in Scottsdale. It was around 10:00 p.m. when I got there. People were getting drunk, but not crazy drunk. I got a request right away. Believe me; it was a mess. Too many people were standing and lining up on the street—either to get inside the bar or just wander outside. I didn't know why so many people congregated outside the bar. Maybe the bar was full, or perhaps they just wanted to be outside. The GPS told me I was 900 ft away, 800ft, 700ft, 600 ft, 400ft…and finally, it said you have arrived. I was at the pickup location. I was looking for someone to come to the car but didn't see anyone. So, I texted the rider. The rider replied, "I'm here."

I asked, "Where?"

The rider said, "I'm here, in front of the bar where people are lining up."

I texted back, "I don't see you."

By texting back and forth, I spent about twenty minutes. Then the rider canceled the ride. Right in the same place, another request came. The GPS showed the same bar. All the people were wearing costumes, and I couldn't differentiate them. Even the area was busy with people, Ubers, and taxis. Again, the rider tried to get hold of me. Still, I didn't see them. I drove back and forth and circled around but still couldn't find the riders. Then, that rider canceled on me, too. It weren't easy even for an experienced driver, let alone a fresh driver like me.

After circling for another forty minutes, I decided to go to a less crowded location. It was a little bit far from the place I was, so Uber gave me another ride. At that point, the surge price was ten times than regular price. I was confident that I would pick up this rider and make good money. Finally, The GPS showed me that it was at the location. I looked around, but I didn't see anyone coming. In this location, the problem was you couldn't stop for more than three or five minutes. There were no parking spots due to heavy traffic— both cars and people. Still, I was looking for the rider, but I couldn't figure out who they were, not when so many people were waiting to pick them up. This rider called me, but we couldn't understand each other. She couldn't understand my English, and I didn't understand hers either because she was drunk and spoke quickly. When I looked out at the crowd, everyone looked the same. This one took me another forty minutes. Currently, the time is around midnight. The rider kept calling to find me, but I didn't know how to tell her where exactly I was except by saying, "I'm here." So, the rider canceled on me again. Right away,

OF COURSE, UNDREAMED

I got another request. This one was far to the south, and the price was fifteen times more than the actual price. I was so desperate. I needed to make this one. I drove to the location, which took me twenty-five minutes. I got there were a bunch of people outside the bar. This time, I called the rider ahead of time. I barely heard him because it was too loud. I asked him where to meet other than the bar to make it easier. He told me he could come towards me a little closer. I thanked him and hung up the phone. I was getting closer to the bar but didn't know where the guy was. After I missed him many times, finally, we found each other. By then, it was 2:00 a.m. It was time for the bars to close. After I dropped the rider off, I decided to go home. I was wasting my gas, mileage, and my energy. The whole night, I only picked up four people and made $150. Isn't that crazy?

I called my friend in the morning to tell him about the previous night's experience. He rushed to find out what I did.

He said,

"How was it?"

I said, "It is devastating."

He said, "How?" I told him how hard it was to find people.

He said, "Sorry." Then he asked me how much I had made. I told him I made $150.

He laughed at me and said, "Which area did you drive in?" I replied that I was working in Scottsdale.

He responded, "You shouldn't go there. The Scottsdale area is hard, even for those with experience, especially on holidays like this. You should call me before you head there." He was still laughing at me and continued, "Anyways, it is okay. You got the experience from it. Even if you don't make that much money." Then, he added, "You know people, make between $500 and $1000 at night. I made $750, which isn't bad."

I felt jealous when he said that, but I didn't spit any words out of my mouth and felt sorry for myself. But at the same time, I felt happy that at least I made some money for my gas. And it was true; I got the experience.
I had even motivated myself to keep driving Uber. I was a fresh Uber driver and always got lost, especially going on the freeways.

One day, I was driving to drop a guy at Sky Harbor airport. I was on Freeway 51 South. I was supposed to keep left on Freeway 51 to exit. I stayed in the middle lane. Mistakenly, I passed the exit. That middle lane took me to I-10 East. The rider was in a hurry. He saw me as I missed the exit. He was so upset with me.
He said, "I'm late for my flight. Where are you going?"

OF COURSE, UNDREAMED

I apologized for missing the exit. I drove two miles east to find another exit to return to the airport. I didn't know how that rider rated me. I was sure he would rate me as an inexperienced driver. The thing is, Uber doesn't tell you who rates you well or who rates you poorly.

I liked driving. I got to know the city more and more, and I got to meet many people. My favorite days to drive Uber were Thanksgiving and Christmas Eve because people moved around frequently and traveled a lot, so I would get frequent requests with surge pricing, and on top of that, people tipped well on the holidays. There were plenty of airport rides and city rides too. But I wouldn't say I liked driving on New Year's Eve and the Fourth of July in Phoenix. People would get drunk on those holidays, and dealing with their attitudes and behaviors weren't very pleasant. Some people were racist, too. Don't get me wrong, plenty of friendly people were out there, too. On the other hand, on the Fourth of July, I want to celebrate freedom too. After all, it's the day of independence. I wanted to celebrate. On the Fourth of July, I hosted a barbeque and invited some friends over to have fun together. We sang and danced to country music, especially listening to the struggle songs. Other than those days, I kept driving Uber whenever I could.

One day, I was in the south Phoenix area and got a request. When I arrived, I saw that the area was a gated community. While waiting for the passenger, one lady approached me with this huge dog. I assumed she was just out walking her dogs. But then I saw her getting closer and closer to me. I suspected something and changed my car gear from P shift to D shift. Right away, she started yelling at me.

She said, "Leave right now. If you don't leave right now, I am going to unleash the dog on you or call the police." I was so shocked and scared, and I hit the gas and disappeared from the area. She even followed me in her car until I was far enough away.

I drove Uber for eight months in Arizona, and I am still driving Uber in Portland, Oregon. For me, driving is fun and crazy. It is an addiction, too. Uber became my only source of income. It was a relief, entertainment, and hobby. My Driving experience and good customer service skills started in Phoenix and moved with me to the gray and rainy city of Portland, which I love.

Chapter Five

Hoyyoo, The Lost Soul

Everything was going smoothly now. I was routinely dropping Obama off with Hoyyo. One day, on a Monday morning, when I picked him up, she gave him candy and rubbed his head. I was confused—she never gave him candy before, and why was she rubbing his head? Had he fallen at night?

I asked, "Is he ok?

She said, "Yes."

Then right when we were leaving,

she said, "I will see you next time if God wills."

I said, "Ok, see you, Hoyyoo." I called her Hoyyoo, which means mom because she was just like my mom.

She treated me like her daughter. She made me tea and bread in the morning when I returned from work to pick up Obama. Still, I wondered what she meant by "If God wills," but I didn't pay attention to her words. I just rushed to leave because my son needed to go to school. We left her on Monday morning.

On Wednesday around noon, someone called me and asked me if I heard about the death around my neighborhood. I said to that person I hadn't anything. That person told me one old lady died of a heart attack yesterday, which was Tuesday morning. I just felt something abnormal run through my body. I felt discomfort in my heart. Maybe I don't like hearing about death. Even now, I don't like hearing about death. I had a feeling in my gut that something was wrong.

I asked, "Who passed away?"

They said, "I don't know her name, but it was one nice Somali lady who is always seen at the mosque." I just hung up the phone, and I rushed to call Hoyyoo. Her daughter answered and said, "Hoyyoo passed away."

I repeated the words loudly. "Passed away?!"

I even had a kind of mini heart attack. My heart stops beating for a second. I faded out for a minute or so. How could I believe that the lady I had said goodbye to her yesterday was dead now? We hoped to see each other on Friday, but now she was gone. I couldn't believe it. Life was too short. I wished in my heart that Hoyyoo hadn't died. I hoped that she was healthy. I had seen her many times walking in the park. She hadn't mentioned to me that she had a heart problem. That was a nightmare. Imagine? Your joy and hope are gone in a single day. No hope, no future. I felt like the whole world had collapsed on me. I had no way to get out.

After refusing and denying the truth, I accepted the fact. I needed to mourn. I needed to go to her house, even though I wouldn't see Hoyyoo, and greet her. At the same time, I didn't want to show my heartbroken feelings and tears to Obama. I needed to hide my pain somehow. Then, I thought ahead to Friday—what was I going to tell him? Was I going to tell him that Hoyyoo passed away? Even if I did him, he would likely not believe me. What would his reaction be? While I struggled with the truth, I knew I needed to go to her house. I called one of my coworkers whom I had a close relationship with and asked him to come to my home and watch Obama for me for a little bit. I didn't tell him what happened, I just asked him to come. He came right away. I waited for him at the door. When I heard him knocking, I opened it and left for Hoyyoo's house.

When I got there, I saw people gathered around, and it finally hit me that Hoyyoo was gone. I cried and cried continuously for a while until her daughter came to me and comforted me. She told me to be strong and asked me to pray for her. I would always pray for

Hoyyoo, and I would never forget her. I cried harder than I ever had in my life, probably more than I would have called if my mom passed away. God snatched from me that gold, kind, and humble lady in the glimpse of an eye. I hated life more and more. I even developed depression and panic attacks. Why was life such a roller coaster for me? It bounced me here and there and everywhere.

Unfortunately, I went back to my complicated life. Again, I had to return to Natsenet, my other friends, and someone I knew through work. Natsenet had already told me that she would not keep him. I didn't know about my other friends. Who else could I talk to? There was no one. I had already begged her before Hoyyoo became my babysitter. I didn't know if Natsenet say ok.

So, until I found the solution, I needed to bring him back to work with me again. I knew I was going to break the work policy again. Still, I didn't have another option. I was scared of facing the people I worked with.

My supervisor had been changed, and I rarely saw the new one. I convinced my co-worker Craig that the last option was to bring him to work like I used to. My babysitter was dead. And until I found a new one, I had no choice but to take him with me. Craig knew how much I hated failing. The only thing he didn't tell me was about shelter. I weren't aware of that at the time. Why hadn't other people told me about it?

OF COURSE, UNDREAMED

I started bringing my son to work with me again. He slept in the car. It was the middle of January. It was not good weather. The temperature was around 45 to 50 degrees at night. It was cold for us. I had to bring three blankets with me—one to spread on the car seat and the other two to cover him from the cold. Most of the time, I left the heater on in the car. When it got hot, I turned it off. I kept taking him with me for a while.

One day, Obama asked me why we stopped going to Hoyyoo's house. I told him that she moved out.

He said, "She didn't tell me."

What could I tell him? Can I say she is dead or what? I tried to hide the truth and told him it was an unexpected sudden move-out. Sudden death is indeed us unexpectedly moving out.

He said, "Where did they move to?"

I said she had moved to Somalia but didn't think he believed me.

He kept asking, "Is Somalia a better place to move?"

I said I didn't know. I couldn't tell him Hoyyoo was dead.

After Hoyyoo died, I developed terrible panic attacks, stress, and anxiety. My neck, shoulder, my chest, and back—my whole body was in pain. My neck and shoulders were very stiff and tight. I couldn't focus on anything.

One day, I was driving on the freeway to go to work. I think it was Freeway 202 North. I felt dizzy and numb while I was driving. God knows what happened to me; I just became dull. Luckily enough, I was close to the exit. I felt dizzy, but with the almighty's help, I hit the brake, and the car stopped moving.

I was pulled over for about fifteen minutes. After a while, I became conscious, but I was still very disoriented. I didn't know where I was or where to go. I called my co-worker and told him I was lost. He guided me on the phone. He told me to put on the four-way flash, slowly drive to the exit, and see what that exit is. I was lucky. It was a Sunday night, and there weren't much traffic on the freeway. I slowly drove to the exit. That exit was the Bellmont exit. I was still disoriented and needed to follow my co-worker's directions. I had been coming from my friend's house who invited us for Christmas. I had left my son Obama with her. I was so lucky he weren't with me. She was a nice friend. She told me that I could leave Obama with them for the night. She even offered me one day to keep Obama with her: Saturday night. The thing was, her house was far from my place, and even further from my workplace. Her house was thirty-five minutes from my house and an hour from my workplace. Still, I did it for a couple of weeks. It was better than nothing.

OF COURSE, UNDREAMED

The pain around my neck and shoulder was getting worse, and my stomach acid reflex was getting worse, too. Every week, I had to go to the emergency room. I thought I was going to die every time I got sick. I was so stressed out and depressed. I lost my appetite. Whatever I ate it gives me a stomach-ache. I developed fear. Even staying in an apartment scared me. I was experiencing anxiety for no reason.

Depression is real—I felt it. I tasted it. I couldn't go to sleep. I was hopeless, scared to go out in public, but at the same time, I was scared to be alone and feel intense loneliness. Everything was dark, and I didn't have a bright future. I didn't want to share my experience with people. I pretended I was normal. I was lucky I had my son with me, who hugged me when I was depressed. He asked me when my face dropped down,

"What happened to you, Emma?" He calls me Emma. I tried to hide from him and pretend that I was okay. Then, something rang in my head. I said to myself,

"Do not lose yourself. Look at your baby. He is your hope." After that, I started praying and doing something that made me feel busy, like cleaning, doing laundry, cooking, going for a walk around the neighborhood, or going to Natsenet's house. When I went to work, my pain got worse.

One day at work, Craig said,

"You may have developed homesickness; you need to visit your family. That might help you."

I said,

"How can I, Craig? I don't have money to get a plane ticket. I can barely pay my bills."

Craig thought to himself for a little while and said,

"I think your stress is from the difficulty of childcare. I know Az-mentor has a day program. You can ask our boss to transfer you there. You know you are risking your and your son's lives too." He continued talking,

"Bringing your child to the workplace at night isn't safe for either of you. Ask the boss if she can ask for you to transfer, or you can ask the office yourself for a transfer.

So, I asked the manager the following day She said,

"Ok, if it works for you." But before that, I needed to ask the day Program manager if he had an open spot.

I said, "Thank you."

She asked the day program manager, who told her he had one open spot. I transferred to the day program. The day program manager was a nice guy; he was from Africa. He understood me better than other people. If I ever asked him if I could go home early or if my son had early release, I would be allowed to go early. I dropped my son off in the morning at school and went to work. I picked him up after work. This shift worked better for me. I regretted not asking people about the Day Program. If I had known, I could transfer early, and I wouldn't have had to struggle this much with my son. Being new to everything is a challenge. Thanks to Craig, I got the shift. Still, I felt hopeless, nothing made me happy, and I got bored easily and irritated easily. I couldn't see bright life in the future, everything was dark for me, and all I could think about was death. That was depression.

Chapter Six

Oregon and Settlement

While I was in this horrible condition, my ex, Hussein Shibo, who is my son's dad, called me from Ethiopia and told me as he was coming to the US for the truck and field competition. He told me he wanted to see his son. Sometimes, he called Obama and spoke to him on the phone.

I asked him, "Where in the US?"

He said, "I am coming to Oregon." I didn't know much about Oregon, but I heard the name before when my friends talked about the Trail Blazers basketball team.

I replied, "Ummm...."

He told me the day he would arrive, and he asked me if I'd be able to meet him in Oregon with Obama. Then he could spend those times with his son while he was in Oregon. I asked him why he couldn't come to Arizona.

He said, "I'm with the Ethiopian athletic team; I can't leave the team; I need to be with them all the time. Sorry, I can't come to Arizona."

I asked, "Why can't you come after the competition?"

He replied that if he stayed behind the team in America after the competition, the officials in Ethiopia might defame him for seeking asylum in the US. He didn't want to hear that. Even at that time, there was political turmoil in Ethiopia.

I said, "So, what do you want me to do?"

He said, "I will pay for your plane ticket and hotel room if you meet me in Oregon."

I replied, "If so, okay."

He added, "I miss my son a lot."

My son always talked about him, too. But sometimes, I stopped communication between Obama and his dada because he always cried after hanging up with him on the phone.

Then the following day, he called me again and told me that he would refund me the money if I booked the flight and hotel.

I said, "Ok."

AMEN MOHAMMED

It was March 16th, 2016. It was around my son's birthday. It was a wonderful opportunity that my son to celebrate his birthday with his dad.

I booked the flight, hotel, and rental car, too. We took an early flight from Phoenix to Portland. Our flight had a connection in LA. We flew with Alaska Airlines. We arrived in LA safely and needed to change the gate for the Portland flight, but we were still on the same airplane. We got to the gate and started boarding right away. All passengers boarded the plane. While the plane was about to take off, the captain announced that the aircraft had some minor issues that needed to be fixed. The technicians were called, and we had to remain in our seats. The captain first announced it would take thirty minutes or less to fix. Thirty minutes passed. The technicians were still coming up and going down. One hour and thirty minutes later, there was still no solution. We were still sitting on the plane at the gate. They still told us to remain seated. Then, two hours and thirty minutes passed, and the crew announced that the aircraft had issues and that we would be moved to another flight. My son and I sat at the back of the plane. They put the people ahead of us on the early flight—it was first come, first serve. By the time we got off the plane, all the flights were full.

So, we needed to wait for the evening flight from LA to Portland. We had broad the plane around 8:30 p.m. We didn't have any option other than to wait for

87

that flight. A customer service agent compensated us with a voucher for lunch and dinner.

After the fifteen-hour delay, we finally made it to Portland. We arrived around 10:00 p.m. Meanwhile, my son's dad arrived in Portland two days earlier. The car rental picks up location weren't at the airport. I needed to wait thirty minutes for a shuttle to come. Finally, after the shuttle came and took us to the car rental place, I picked up the car and started driving to the hotel. By then, it was 11:00 p.m. I'd booked a room at the Econo Lodge in the Milwaukie area. While I was driving towards the hotel, the GPS stopped working. I lost the signal. I didn't know where to go without the GPS. My son became frustrated and started crying. He said, "You brought me here to perish me? We don't know the city, and we don't know anyone here. How can we find our way to the hotel?''

I told him to calm down. I assured him that I was not trying to perish him. I told him it would be ok and that I would figure it out. To be honest, I was becoming very panicked, but I didn't want to show him that. In the middle of the night, I was in a new and unfamiliar city, and the GPS was not working. Crazy. After I got lost many times on the road, the GPS started working, and we finally arrived at the hotel. Wow!

When my signal returned, I saw a lot of missed calls from my son's dad. After I got our luggage and checked in, I called him. He told me he had been worried.

My son's father was staying at the Hilton Hotel in downtown Portland. He wanted us to meet him at his hotel right away. I told him we were tired and couldn't come immediately. I told him we would see him in the morning.

He insisted and said, "I want to see my son. You don't know how I missed him!"

I asked my son if he wanted to go to his father's hotel.

He said, "No. We will get lost again; thus, I don't want to go, plus I am tired now. I will see him in the morning." Brave kid!

I told his dad that we were both very tired and Obama was already sleepy. I told him once more that we'd see him in the morning.

We woke up in the morning at around 11:00 a.m. I had a lot of missed calls from my son's dad again. I took a shower, and so did Obama. We ate breakfast and headed to the Hilton Hotel.

Father and son saw each other for the first time since we left Ethiopia. They were both excited to see each other. But Obama's father's excitement weren't higher than his father's. I think the situation that happened on the way to Portland may have affected my son's mood—the flight delay and getting lost while driving in the middle of the night made him less excited. Still, his father was his father, and they hugged, kissed, and enjoyed each other's presence.

My son always asked me why his father weren't around like the other children's fathers. I always told him he would see him one day. This was the day my son had been waiting for a long time. I could see his face light up with happiness when he saw his father.

We all stayed together during the daytime, and then Obama and I left for our hotel in the late evening. We did this throughout the trip, but my son stayed with his father for one night—other than that, he was always with me because he was mommy's boy!

On one occasion, we get to meet some old friends of my son's father. They asked us where we lived, and I told them Phoenix, Arizona.

Everybody said, "It is too hot. How could you live somewhere so hot?''

I said, "Yes. I know."

Then they said, "Why you don't move here then?" They continued, "It's good here. The weather is good; you will find a job easily; there are a lot of opportunities here; even you can start your own business." Then, they mentioned some Ethiopian people who owned a business. "You can be like them, too."

Honestly, I was starting to feel better since I arrived in Portland. No pain, no stress. I started laughing. I felt relieved; my neck and shoulders became loose, and I felt like a big load had dropped from my shoulder.

Everybody I met in Portland said, "You better move here." My son even met some friends and celebrated his birthday with them. In general, it was a nice mini vacation for us.

I loved the weather and the greenery. It was spring in Portland. I could smell fresh flowers. It was time for the Japanese Cherry Blossoms to bloom. The smell was in the air everywhere. Everywhere was green. It was soul healing. I felt it, and I got connected to nature. I thought that nature was so beautiful in Oregon when I was there. It would rain for a bit and then stop, and then the sun would come out, then it would rain again, then stop again, and then the sun would come out. Perhaps it was a bit cold for us for Phoenix people—when we were there, the temperature in Phoenix was eighty-eight or ninety degrees, and it was forty-five degrees in Portland. Finally, after five days, it was time to go back to Phoenix. My son didn't want to leave Portland.

He said, "I don't want to go to Phoenix. I want to stay with my father and my friends in here."

I told him his father was going back to Ethiopia.

Then he said, "I will stay with my friends."

I told him we couldn't just stay in Portland without any plan. I told him we needed to bring our stuff and car, and I needed a job to move to Portland. And I promised him that I would work on it, and by summer, I would get things ready, and we would move to Portland. After refusing a couple of times, he agreed to go back to Phoenix, at least for the time being. To be honest, I hated the idea of going back to Phoenix.

Right after we returned to Arizona, I started searching for three things in Portland: rent, job, and childcare. I didn't want to mess up with childcare and suffer again. At least I had a convenient working schedule for my son now. I kept searching. Finally, I found the DHS office that assisted with childcare in Oregon. And I kept searching for rent too. Luckily, I found a good option and filled out the application online. In addition, I was searching for a job too. While I was looking for a job in Portland, I asked my supervisor if Az-mentor had a branch in Portland.
He said, "I will ask for you."

The next day, he came with the good news that Az-mentor had an Oregon mentor branch in Portland. It looked like things were going in the right direction for me. Then, all I needed to do was to make sure I found an apartment, a job, and childcare before I decided to move. In the meantime, the apartment manager called me fifteen days after I had submitted my application and told me there was an apartment that would be ready in the first week of June. I replied that I was ok with that. Then, my boss found me the

OR-Mentor number. I called them. I talked to one person, and he said they were ok with the transfer, but it had to be done through my manager in Phoenix. I didn't want to waste time, so I went to the office the next day and asked my manager if she could submit the transfer request for me. She asked me why I wanted to transfer. I told her because of family, which was a lie. She submitted the request right away, then after a couple of days, they accepted my transfer. The only thing left was childcare. I called one of my ex's friends and asked about childcare government assistance. She told me about many programs that helped with childcare.

She said, "Don't worry about it; if you decide to come, just come."

With that, I got the assurance I needed.

My lease in Phoenix was set to end on May 31st. If I renewed it, I would have to stay in Phoenix for another six months. At the same time, I didn't want to be in Phoenix in the coming summer. I contacted the apartment lady to make sure the apartment would be ready in June. She told me it would be ready between June 6th and 10th by then. I didn't want to make the mistake I made when I moved to Iowa. After I got assurance from her, I decided to move.

I decided to take all my belongings with me— everything in my house. Everything! So, I needed to find a moving company within two months. I searched for moving companies, and they were so expensive. Finally, I found one which was affordable. And I realized that I needed to ship my car too. I couldn't drive now as I did in Iowa. I didn't have a good relationship with Esme then. I didn't want to involve him. I needed to pack all my furniture, including a bed and sofa. I needed to plan for pick-up. I needed to book our flight to Portland. And the last thing I needed to do was to find a hotel for ten days until my apartment was ready.

I also needed to tell Esme that we were moving before the day we were leaving. I texted him to come to my house after work. I think it was May 15th, 2016. I asked his advice when I moved to Iowa. But now, we weren't in that situation. I knew for sure that when I told him I was moving away, he was not going to say anything. I was ready to move on. Before he came, I prepared coffee and made dinner—rice and chicken. Esme loved my rice. When he got to my apartment, he noticed something was off but didn't want to say anything. Some of my stuff weren't there anymore because I had already started packing. After he had dinner and coffee, we chatted for a little bit. Then, I told him I was moving. He knew he couldn't change my mind. He also knew he weren't as supportive as he promised. I told him I had already finished the packing and showed him around.

I could see two emotions running down his face. One was guilty of not keeping his promise to support us, and the other was happy that I was moving on. He knows there weren't a strong bond between us anymore.

Finally, he said, "I'm happy for you. I wish you the best wherever you go. And I'm sorry I could not fulfill my promises."

I said, "It's ok. It weren't meant for us to be together. I know you are not a decision-making person in nature, and you take your time, and I don't know when that time will be. I can't wait forever. I'm not even sure if you will decide to live with me. So, I need to move on. Esme." I then added, "I think both of us are looking for better opportunities, to be honest, especially me."

He shook his head and said, "I'm not looking for opportunity."

I said, "I am." That was kind of rough!

"Anyway, I wish you the best," he said.

I replied, "Thank you. I wish you the same."

He said, "I will come the day the moving company comes and help you with loading stuff," but when moving day arrived, he never came. Disappointing!

It was June 1st, 2016. It was a beautiful time of year, between spring and summer. It was still green, fresh, and flourishing. Obama and I landed at Portland airport around noon. One of my ex-husband's friends

OF COURSE, UNDREAMED

Midhaksa gave us a ride to the Howard Johnson Hotel. The hotel was on NE 82nd and Sandy BLV. While we were taking showers, Midhaksa left us to bring us lunch. He brought us fast food.

I don't remember exactly what it was. He left us and told us that he would come tomorrow for lunch. After we ate, I slept around four p.m. while Obama was watching TV in our bedroom. I was so tired from preparing, packing, and loading all the boxes of my stuff for moving out. I was knocked out. I don't know what time Obama went to sleep. The hotel had breakfast. I woke up around five a.m. and went back to sleep again. Finally, we both woke up at nine a.m. and went to breakfast. Breakfast was served between six am to ten a.m. We ate our breakfast and came back to our room. We were both happy to have left Phoenix. (By the way, when I moved out, Natsenet was in Ethiopia, but Zaru, her husband, was still in Phoenix. He was the only person who helped me clean the old apartment; then, I could return the key for an uncleaned apartment without charge.

For a couple of days, Obama and I were in the hotel by ourselves. We ate breakfast late, so we would be full for the whole day. I had snacks with me that I had brought from Phoenix for dinner. I just gave him a snack when he said he was hungry. What we did for the whole day was eat breakfast, go back to the room, or go to the swimming pool inside the hotel. On one occasion, while walking around the hotel, I saw a restaurant, Namaste Indian, in front of the hotel. We went there for dinner a couple of times while we stayed at the hotel. They had a buffet. It looked like a vacation for us. I have never gone on a vacation since arriving in the US, except when we came to

Portland to meet my son's father three months ago.

One day, I received a call from a stranger. It was a young lady who called me and introduced herself. She said,

"My name is Bontu, and one of your ex-husband's friends told me you are staying in a hotel alone."

I told her, "That is exactly right."

She said, "Where and what hotel are you at? What is the name of the hotel?"

I said, "Howard Johnson."

She asked, "Which one?"

I said, "The one on NE 82nd and Sandy BLV."

She said, "Oh, wow, that is in my neighborhood. You are in my neighborhood." She laughed.

I laughed back. We didn't even know each other.

She said,

"Okay, I will come and say hi to you within thirty minutes. Can you text me the room number?"

I said, "Ok," but I thought it was strange. After I hung up the phone, I was thinking about her and what kind of person she was. Meanwhile, I texted the room number.

She came exactly thirty minutes later and knocked on the door. For the most part, I didn't believe she would come immediately.

I opened the door, and she came in. She hugged me first; then she greeted my son. Right away, Obama started asking,

"Who is she?" I told him she was my friend.

Then he said,

"How come you didn't tell me about her before?"

Then, after she sat for a couple of minutes at the edge of our bed, she said,

"Let's go to my house, and we can chat for a little bit, and then I'll bring you back to your hotel,"

Obama asked her if she had a kid. She told him she did.

Then, he said,

"Do you have a basketball hoop?"

She said,

"Yes," we left the hotel and went to her house. It was only a two-minute drive from our hotel to her house.

Obama was eight years old by now. He was so excited to play basketball.

I think God sent us this woman. She made us yummy food and coffee. We ate, chatted, and had fun together as if we had known each other for a while, like we were best friends who had reunited. The truth was, I was a stranger to her, and she was a stranger to me too, but our conversation and situation didn't look that way. What connected us was one commonality— the single mom thing. The struggle, the difficulty. Once upon a time, she was in the same situation as me.

Out of the ten days we stayed at the hotel, I think we spent four at her house. She worked Monday to Friday. Saturday and Sunday were her days off. We were together on those two days.

My car came before my other belongings arrived. My apartment was ready by now to move in. I just grabbed my luggage from the hotel and went to my apartment. Luckily, I had some extra blankets in my luggage and my car. We slept on the floor and ate out until all my cooking utensils arrived. In the meantime, I was looking for summer programs and government daycare assistance for my son. While I was searching for both, I found one called the YMCA. I googled to find the number for the YMCA. I found it. Then, I called them. The operator transferred me to the program coordinator. The program coordinator asked me who she was talking to. I told her my full name.

OF COURSE, UNDREAMED

Then she said, "How may I help you?"

I told her I had moved recently to Portland and was looking for a daycare my son could attend while I went to work. She told me I was lucky because only one open spot was available. If I hadn't called today, that open spot probably would have been gone by tomorrow. Then she told me what I needed to do before they accepted me.

The first thing I needed to do was apply. Then, they would review the application and contact me if they needed more information.

Right after I finished with her, I googled the nearest library because my apartment didn't have Wi-Fi. I found the nearest one, which was Rockwood Library. I drove there and applied.

The lady had already emailed me the form. In the meantime, we signed up for membership at the library. My son got all *The Dairy of Whimpey Kid* books and some other books from there. I missed going to that place!

The appointment day was Wednesday. It was around 1:30 p.m. in Selam. I took my son with me. I didn't know how far Selam was until the GPS said an hour and fifteen minutes. I just wanted to get some help for my son so he could be there while I was gone from work. I didn't even mind driving that far until my friend Bontu told me that Selam was very far.

She said, "How could you drive from here to Selam? You just got here two weeks ago. I lived in Portland for a long time and never drove to Selam."

We laughed. I told her I didn't mind driving because I was an Uber driver back in Phoenix. An hour of driving was nothing for me. She was so amazed that I was driving to Selam. The only thing I needed to do when I drove in a new area was use the GPS.

After a couple of days, the YMCA coordinator called me and told me they were reviewing my application and would let me know via email if I was approved for the program. She said, "Expect the email within three to four days." She was a nice lady and wished me good luck with my new life.

Everything happened so fast. After three days, the same lady called me and said, "Congratulations! You are approved for the program." She explained to me about the YMCA and the summer program. The program ran from late June to mid-August. It was from Monday to Friday. It started at 7:00 a.m. and ended at 5:00 p.m. The place they assigned me was Vernon elementary school.

I also went to the OR-Mentor's office to ask them to assign me the closest area in consideration of my son's summer program. As I mentioned earlier, I did finish the job transfer process while in Phoenix. Back then, they told me they would assign me the location when I got to Portland. I needed to go to the OR-

OF COURSE, UNDREAMED

Mentor's office to get assigned to the day program. I went to the office one day after I dropped Obama off at the YMCA. The daycare manager, Donna, took me to her office. Then she offered me two locations I could choose from. One had a lot of clients, and the other not that many. I chose the one with fewer people because caregiving is not easy. Everyone at least needs some help from you. Sometimes you run out of time and energy. If you don't take care of everybody when they get home, the group of home people will complain about you. The place I chose was a little bit far from my son's summer program. At that point, I didn't even know the city very well. I told Donna that the place I chose was a little bit far from my son's daycare.

She said, "Where is your son's place?"

I told her the address.

She said, "Oh, it is close to MLK Day program. I will see if we have any openings there."

Right away, she contacted the supervisor over there. The supervisor told her that one caregiver was leaving soon, and they needed someone to replace them.

Donna said,

"We have many clients there, but there are four caregivers who work at that place. You would not be by yourself. They will help you."

I agreed and accepted the spot.

I dropped my son at the YMCA at 7:30 a.m. at Vernon elementary school and went to work. Vernon and my workplace weren't far from each other. It was about a ten-minute drive. I picked him up at 4:00 p.m. Sometimes, I picked him up late. The program costs $250 a week. I needed to contribute $51 a week. I was happy, but I didn't know I needed to contribute that money until the supervisor at Vernon School told me. Still, it was better for me. My son was even happy being there. He participated in different activities, like outdoor activities and swimming, that he never did in Arizona.

Finding that place for my son while I was working was a big relief. In Portland, I finally didn't have to beg people to take care of him that much. I didn't know anyone except a few people, including Bontu. I liked the change very much, and so did my son, too. Still, we spent Saturday and Sunday with Bontu. Sometimes, we slept over.

The YMCA program ended in the middle of August. They gave me the notice for the last day. So, I needed to find a new daycare. I have already applied for daycare assistance at DHS, and I am waiting for their response. The next day, after I picked up my son from the YMCA, I went to the DHS office to ask about my case. The front desk lady asked me for my case number, and when I gave it to her, she told me to be seated until the case worker called me. Then, the case worker called my number. She took me inside with her. She pointed me to sit on the chair in front of her. She looked at my case and said, "Why is it pending while it is already approved?" She continued, "You are eligible for a copay."

I asked her what she meant.

She explained to me what it meant to receive a co-pay for my son's daycare. The government would pay some money for the daycare provider, and I need to pay the rest. Now, I understood, and I agreed to pay the copay.

She said, "You need to find childcare. I will give you the list of some providers. You can choose from them or find your childcare provider too." She added, "Here is the list," and handed me a paper with a lot of pages. She continued, "Let us know when you decide. Don't forget to contact us right away when you find one, or else your case will be delayed."

I agreed, and I left with a paper with a lot of pages. I started glancing at them while I was driving home. It was a lot of information.

I called Bontu right when I got home to tell her the good news. This was a miracle for me. I never had government assistance when I was in Phoenix. The whole five years I lived in Phoenix, I was on the waiting list. While Bontu and I were talking about childcare, she said, "I know one lady who does childcare at her home. She is from our community; she has a license from the DHS. I will ask her and tell you what she said, or I will give you her number, then you can contact her."

I preferred contacting her myself, so Bontu gave me the number.

I called the lady right away. She answered the phone. I asked her if she did childcare as if I didn't know that she did.

She said, "Yes, I do." The funny thing was, Bontu already told her I was looking for childcare.

She said, "Are you the one Bontu told me about? Who has just moved from Arizona?"

I replied, "Yes."

She added, "Welcome; how is everything? Did you settle yet?"

I said, "I am trying."

She told me she would help me with what she could. Then we talked for a while about everything, about life in Phoenix, back home, and so on, as if we had known each other for a long time. (By the way, I don't have problems with communication. I can get along with people easily, except Rabirra.)

Another day, I called the DHS case worker to let her know, as she was my provider. I started dropping my son off with her after the YMCA program ended. Still, life was treating me well. All my pain and stress were lessening. In Portland, I had a new life and renewed hope.

When school started, I enrolled Obama at Margaret Scott Elementary School. I dropped him off in the morning at the bus stop, and after school, my childcare provider would pick him up from there.

On the other hand, life in Oregon was not as cheap as in Arizona. The rent was double here. So, I needed to find a second job to keep up with life. I decided to work on weekends. Then, I could pay all my bills. I found a cashier position at The Home Depot. My son stayed with a childcare provider those days. Sometimes, I took him to Bontu.

The day program job is becoming harder. Two caregivers had quit. Only two of us took care of twelve clients in the morning and twelve in the afternoon. The morning shift was from 8:30 a.m. to noon. The afternoon shift was from 12:30 p.m. to 3:30 p.m. The job was so tiring and hectic. All the clients needed full assistance, like feeding, changing, and helping with the restroom. Most of the time, I helped feed two to three clients simultaneously. When my shift ended, I was always beaten up, tired, and exhausted. I didn't want to stay there for a long time. I started looking for a better and less heavy job.

Chapter Seven

Tri-met Lift Driving and Bad Luck

I got to know one tri-met lift driver when he dropped off a client. One day, I asked him what his driving job was like.

He said, "It is nice."

I told him I was tired of my job. He told me I could apply for a tri-met lift. He gave me the website. I filled out the application at home the very same day.

After a week or so, they called me for an interview. I spoke to the same guy before they called me for an interview. He told me what their interview looked like. I was prepared. The interview went great, and I got the job. They hired me! The whole process took around two weeks. I needed to give two weeks' notice at my job.

The tri-met lift was operated by First Transit Company. They gave transportation services to people with disabilities. I think the state covered their transportation expenses or they paid a small amount of money for each trip. Tri-met lift bus was not one of those big ones. It was medium in size bus.

Before I started driving the bus, I needed to complete five weeks of training and pass the test by at least eighty-five percent. Then I needed to do the hands-on training for two weeks and pass that too. The safety test was especially important. I needed to know most of the outside bus conditions and some parts of the engine compartment. On the outside, I needed to know about the headlights, the backlight, the wheels, the rim, and the tire. When it came to the hood compartment, I needed to know about the serpentine belt, oil level, some bolts, and the engine. Inside the bus, I needed to know how to tie the wheelchair and make sure the holding bars were intact. I needed to know how to park the bus in parallel parking. I hated the parking test. It included five different parking types. On top of that, I needed to pass the CDL test and medical exam.

I started the class on October 3rd, 2016. As I said, it took me five weeks of class training and two weeks of hands-on training. In short, I completed all the training and passed the test and CDL. I still worked at The Home Depot on Saturdays and Sundays.

Finally, to start driving myself, I needed to do the co-dating, which is someone would sit next to me and evaluate my driving for two weeks. If the co-date person approved of my driving, I would start driving the bus myself. Primarily, they evaluated safety and customer service.

On a Wednesday, it was my first day driving the bus with someone next to me. Of course, I did drive the bus when I did training. Now, this was different. This was a real job. It was an actual job, with real driving on the street around so many cars, people, and bikes. The person who was co-dating me was waiting for me. I went to the schedule board to look for my bus, route, and key. I came back to the key pick-up office, which is at the dispatch office. I picked up the key and told the co-date I was ready. He came with me to the bus. I needed to inspect it before I drove the bus.

I opened the door to expose the engine compartment before I started the bus. I looked for any leakage, checked the oil level and my best friend, the scrpentlne belt, and looked around for any abnormalities. It looked good. Then I closed the hood and jumped onto the bus. I started the engine while I was there, and I checked for my seatbelt tears and if it will be fastened and unfastened properly. I checked the seat itself to see if it moved forward and backward.

OF COURSE, UNDREAMED

And I was looking for any malfunction of the seat. Further, I looked at the dashboard for any light signals and checked the windshield and wipes. I looked for any cracks on the windshield. I checked to see if the mirror operated and moved in the way I wanted to adjust it. Everything looked normal. Then, I jumped out of the bus and started looking for any cracks on the bus. Nothing. I needed to lie down on the ground to see if there was any leakage on the ground under the bus. No leakage. I checked the gas tank and the lid to see if it closed tightly. Then I went to the tires. I checked all the tires for any damage and cracks on the rim.

I checked for tire depth. I came back inside the bust to check if the wheelchair fasting belts were working, if the holding bar was intact on the floor, and checked for any fluid or dirt on the ground. All were ok. Still, the co-date was going up and down, back, and forth, and circling with me around the bus. All inspections were done, and now the bus was ready to drive.

He said, "Good job."

The entire routine took me thirty minutes.

Now, I needed to take the bus from the back parking lot. I needed to back out to get out of the parking spot. I honked a couple of times to make sure nobody was in my way. I needed to make sure there weren't a person or another bus behind me while I was backing up.

Finally, I left the building with my co-date sitting next to me. I was so excited. We headed to my first pick-up location. I got there by following the GPS route. I picked up a lady with a wheelchair. I tied her wheelchair in the wheelchair spot and then started driving towards my second pickup. While I was driving towards the pickup location, my co-date started confusing me with the GPS. He told me to go a different route than the GPS route. He rushed me to turn into the next street, but I was very close to the left lane. So, I needed to rush to change lanes and go to the right lane. It was a very narrow street. He continued rushing me by saying,

"Turn right here, turn right." I was getting nervous when his tone became loud. On the other hand, the GPS was telling me to turn right on 18th Street. But he was rushing me to turn right on 20Th to Couch Street. While I was turning right, a big semi-truck was coming toward me. I was scared, and I thought that truck would hit me. I just gave a little space to the track to pass me. On the other side, my right side, I didn't see the parked cars on the street. I accidentally scraped the bumper of the first car. I heard a cracking sound. My co-date said,

"You hit somebody's car," and then I stopped in the middle of the street. I was so panicked. He got out of the bus and looked around. Our bus was okay, but the other car was scratched on the bumper. Then, he rushed me again to get out of the road because I was blocking traffic. I was so terrified by now. Then, I started moving the bus again, but I scraped another parked car on the side. OMG! Now everything was terrifying me.

The co-date started yelling at me.

"Stop the bus somewhere out of the street!"

Finally, I stopped the bus. Then he paged dispatch. They called us right away. He reported the accident. I was so terrified by the situation. I couldn't talk clearly. Then, the dispatch people reported to the safety office. They told me to stay there until the safety people came. The safety came after a while. I was on the bus, crying. The co-date was standing outside, and the lady on the bus was talking loudly. She seemed confused. The safety people looked around, took note of the surroundings, and asked me what happened. The other bus came to get the lady from this one. Then, the lady left.

Finally, they told me I could go home. I explained that my car was at the office. They said,

"You can go with us." On the way to the office, no one said anything to me until we got inside.

One person said,

"We will investigate the accident and let you know what we decide. Until then, you'll stay home." It sounded like I had committed a crime when he used to word 'investigate.' I knew in my gut that they were going to fire me. I got into my car and was crying until I got home. My eyes became red and swollen. Even my son noticed it and asked why my eyes looked like that. I told him I was having an allergic reaction.

I knew for sure that they were going to fire me. The workers union couldn't fight for me either because I didn't pass my ninety days. So, I was in empty air.

In a panic, I was thinking about what I could do—what job I could start right away. I couldn't wait until they notified me of their decision. I needed to hurry up—the bills were coming. I was in an even worse position because I had been in an accident on November 16th, 2016, in the middle of the month. I didn't have enough money to pay my next month's bills. So, I needed to hurry up and figure out what job I could start right away. After thinking thoroughly for long hours, I came up with the idea of driving for Uber in Portland. If I did it right away, I could cover some of my bills, especially the rent. "This is a good idea," I said to myself. I approved of my idea.

Then, the same night, I planned to go to the Uber hub in Portland in the morning after I dropped my son off. I went to the office. They asked me for my car year. I told them it was a Nissan Murano, 2004. They told me that my car was too old to drive Uber. I needed a car that was ten years old or less. Mine was over ten years old. I left there, hopeless. I could start to feel another headache forming. What could I do? If I were to apply for any job, I wouldn't even start working immediately. It can take two weeks to months to secure a position. I needed something immediately. I asked The Home Depot human resource manager if she could give me more hours.

She said,

"Sorry, unfortunately, we don't have any open shifts right now. All shifts are full. If we have one, I will give it to you. Even if someone calls off, I will give you that, too. Trust me; you are in my priority."

Oh God, I needed to do something right now or in the next couple of days. I started panicking more. It was hard. I have always hated asking people for money. I would have rather died. I started losing hope again. I was beginning to hate my life again. I hated being failed. I didn't want to share my difficulties with people who didn't know me. I didn't want to experience the difficulty I had experienced in Phoenix. I asked myself, "Where are my hope and wishes?"

Nothing could come out of my brain. My brain had shut itself off. I couldn't come up with a solution. I just said, "That's it!

After a lot of deep thinking, I came up with one idea. It involved getting a new car and driving for Uber. This idea seemed to work well in my emergency. In the morning, I went to Ron Tonkin's Toyota after I dropped my son off at school. I headed to the sales department. Right away, one guy from the sales department came to me and said, "Welcome to Ron Tonkin's! How can I help you, ma'am?"

 "I'm looking to buy a car," I said as if I had the money to buy a car.

He said,

"That is wonderful. Let's go to the office and look for the car options we have; then, you can choose." Without pausing, he continued, "Do you have a car you like in mind?"

I said,

"Yes. Toyota Prius." Given its mileage, I knew a Toyota Prius would be perfect for driving for Uber.

We stepped into his office. He gestured for me to sit in the chair in front of him. His computer monitors covered half of his face. I sat there. He asked me again about the car type and the year. I told him about a Toyota Prius that was less than ten years old.

He said,

"Yes. I have plenty of them. You can choose from them." He added,

'"Are you financing or trading?"

I said,

"I don't have money for the down payment."

OF COURSE, UNDREAMED

He said,

"So, you can do trading."

I replied that I didn't want to trade my Nissan. I have a lot of memories of this car. I wanted to keep it.

He said,

"If you have a good credit score, you can do financing. First, let's check your credit score."

I interrupted him and asked what that meant. I was confused. I never did anything with credit before. I was also excited about the outcome at the same time, and I wished for a good credit score.

He said,

"Tell me your social security number I can run your credit history."

I told him my SSN, and he put it in the system. He turned the computer's face towards me so I could see it. He ran the credit. Both of us were so excited to see the score.

The credit report came from two places: Equifax and Trans Union. They both showed low credit scores.

He said,

"I'm sorry, you can't be approved with this low score to finance the car unless you make a big down payment." Again, more heart-breaking news. My hope was gone. I couldn't say anything for a moment. I felt like some heavy object had struck my stomach. I started clenching my teeth. The guy noticed my emotion and offered me a cup of water. I just finished it with one sip. I thanked him for the water. He was a nice guy. Everything looked like a nightmare to me.

He said, "I know you want the car badly. Unfortunately, it didn't happen. You never know; it might be for a good reason." He paused for a moment to hear from me, but I couldn't say anything.

He continued by saying,

"By the way, why do you need the car badly? I'm just curious?"

I said,

"I need the car badly for business," I explained to him why I needed it. I could see his empathy. He asked me if I had a friend. I told him as I had one.

Then he said,

"Bring your friend either today or tomorrow, and your friend will be your co-signer. Then you will approve for finance. After that, you will get the car."

"Oh God, who is going to be my co-signer?" I needed to think. I didn't want to bring Bontu because I didn't want to see her reaction when I told her, and at the same time, I didn't want to hear her say no because that might upset me. So, I decided that I weren't going to bother asking her. Who else could I bring as a co-signer? I was getting frustrated. I didn't want to lose this chance. I already told Bontu as I had gotten into an accident at the Tri-met lift. She even asked her workplace if they had an open shift for me. They told her they didn't have one.

After thinking for a while, someone comes to mind. Midhaksa. He even promised my ex last time to help me when I needed help. Of course, he helped me with many things when I moved here. He gave me a ride from the airport to my hotel and helped me with unloading my stuff from the moving truck when it arrived.

So, I called him and told him I needed him for an emergency. I told him to come right away. He was worried.

He asked, "Are you ok?"

I said,

"Yes, I am ok. Just come right now. I need your help, Midhaksa."

"Is Obama, ok?" he asked.

I replied to him,

"Yes, he is okay. Just come, please!"

He said,

"Where are you?"

I told him that I was at Ron Tonkin's Toyota.

"Where?" he repeated as he didn't hear me.

I said again,

"Ron Tonkin's Toyota."

"What are you doing over there?" he said.

I said,
"Don't question too much. Just come."

He said,

"Okay, I will be there soon. I'm already on my way." He thought I was involved in an accident. He was so nervous. Right when he got to the parking lot and got out of his car, I saw him looking for me. I walked towards him and greeted him. He repeated the same words, "Are you ok?"

I told him I was ok. Then I bowed to his knee and started crying. I held his leg down tightly, and I started sobbing. "Please, Midhaksa help me. Help me." He was so confused about my situation. He lifted me from his knee by holding my two hands. It looked like I was bowing to ask him to marry me.
He said, "Tell me what happened."

I said, "When I tell you the whole story, don't turn your back on me, please." I was begging him and crying at the same time. "Please say ok." I could see that I was putting him in an uncomfortable situation.

He said, "I will say ok, but first, what is it? Just tell me what happened."

OF COURSE, UNDREAMED

We were still in the parking lot. Unwillingly, my tears were still running down my cheeks. My eyes were like a river full of water flowing downstream. I couldn't control my emotions. Everything flashed back to me. Finally, after so much crying, I told him the whole thing and what happened.

He felt sorry for me. He asked me what kind of help I needed from him, and he said,

"I'm willing to help you. Remember, last time Hussein even asked me to help you when you needed help? I got assurance from him."

With too much fear, I asked him if he could be my co-signer to buy a car. I could tell I was putting him in a hard situation; thus, he didn't want to say yes or no.

After quiet silence, he said, "Yes, I don't want to leave you in this situation."

We headed to the same guy inside the dealership who told me to bring a friend to co-sign.

He was with another customer. We needed to wait for him until he was done with the customer. After he was done, he came to us and greeted us. He took us to his office. Right away, he requested our SSN. We both handed him our SSN cards. He put the SSN on the computer. The approval notice came right away.

He congratulated us on the approval. Then, he took us outside, where the cars were parked. We started looking for the options that the salesman gave us. Midhaksa recommended I get Toyota Prius V. Because it is suitable for Uber—it doesn't consume a lot of gas because it is a hybrid. I liked the burgundy color, but Medhaksa preferred the black one.

He said, "Burgundy isn't common in Uber; black is common and good for Uber. Plus, the burgundy gets dirty very often." He continued,

"You know, a black car is a luxury car too."

He convinced me, and I changed my choice to the black Prius V. As it turned out, that was the only Prius V model left in the dealer's compound.

The salesman said, "That is a good choice."

The salesperson brought the key for me to drive it around and see if I liked it. I drove around and discovered that it was an easy car. I liked it.

He took us back to his office to finish the paperwork and complete the transaction. Everything was finished, and I took the car with me by thanking Midhaksa. Finally, I was experiencing relief. Big, big, significant relief. I was thankful for Midhaksa, and I owed him a lot.

The following day, I dropped my son off at school and returned to the Uber office downtown with my new Toyota Prius V 2014 with low mileage. The customer service agent finished everything for me right away. I was already in the system, so there was no need to sign up for a new Uber account. He just updated my address and the car. Even the inspection was quick. My background check came back clear on the same day. I was ready to be on the road.

I started driving the next day after I dropped my son off at school. I drove until my son's pickup time. It weren't bad as the first time driving in a new city, despite the GPS sometimes taking me to a dead end. My driving experience in Phoenix helped me a lot with manipulating the GPS around and finding the riders easily.

Now, I was in better condition. I drove Uber eight to ten hours a day. Thankfully, I was able to pay my bills.

Still, I kept my Saturday and Sunday shifts at the Home Depot job, just in case. It looked like things were working all right, at least for right now.

One day, when I was picking up my son from my childcare provider lady, she told me that she weren't going to do childcare anymore.

She said, "Hold on, Amane, I want to tell you something. Sorry, I won't do childcare anymore. I'm going to stop the job very soon." Something got stuck in my throat. I couldn't say anything.

She continued, "Sorry Amane, I am pregnant. It is hard for me to deal with children."

I didn't want to hear that. I just tried to refuse the information. I said, "What?" As if I didn't hear what she had been saying.

She was annoyed with my nonresponse.

Then, I asked her when she was going to stop the business.

She said, "Starting next month, meaning January."

I said, "What?" loudly again! As if she had done something to me before.

She was confused about my situation.

After that, I didn't want to stand next to her. I just rushed my son out of there and went to my brand-new car to cry. I didn't want to cry in front of her. At the same time, I didn't want to cry in front of my son, either. I just wanted to be home, lock myself in the bathroom, and let my tears flow. I was so devastated by the news.

I live close to the daycare, and I got home right away, then went to the bathroom and let my tears flow. I cried and cried. After I let out my emotion, I started questioning God.

I said, "God, why do you test me badly every time? When will my life be restful? My life is a rollercoaster; there are a lot of ups and downs. I am tired of it. When I say it is over, you bring me another thing. God, am I, not your creature? Why do you do this to me? Please guide me to something better. I'm tired of looking at people's faces. God, I want to know if you are happy with this. I know you don't want to betray me, but you are testing me hard. Do you think I will pass all these tests?"

When I spoke to him, I felt like I connected with him and was talking to him directly. After I spoke to him for a while, I felt something heavy drop from my shoulders. I felt lighter. It was delightful. I got a kind of assurance—that tests are good, that challenges are good. If I passed them, then my future would be bright. So, I wiped my tears, washed my face with warm water, and came out of the bathroom. Obama was watching TV. I was so hungry, but my appetite was gone.

Earlier, before I came to pick up Obama while I was driving Uber, I was thinking about getting something to eat, but I changed my mind about getting it after I picked up Obama. Then this happened. My hunger was gone. I just felt weak and exhausted. I changed my son into his PJs and went to bed.

But I couldn't go to sleep. I needed to think about what I would do after December 31st. Where would I take Obama? I got up in the middle of the night and started staring at the providers list that the DHS case worker had given me. I kept looking and looking at the different providers, comparing their availability and location. Most of them did school time and after-school childcare. Some of them only accepted children under five years of age. So, I couldn't solve my problem. I just threw the paper on the ground and went back to bed, but I still couldn't sleep.

Finally, I came up with the idea of doing Uber early in the morning while Obama was sleeping, during school while he was at school, and after school, while he was at school.

I already applied for the afterschool program, and he was approved. Then, I needed to tell Obama that he weren't going to go to the lady's house anymore. I told him, but he didn't ask me for further explanation. I was happy he didn't ask.

Now, I needed to figure out how I would communicate with him when I left him home. I didn't want to get him a phone because I was scared, he might call 911 for fun or he might call accidentally and get me in trouble. I was scared even thinking about what would happen. So, I needed to figure out different means of communication.

Finally, I came up with the idea of opening a Facebook and Messenger account so I could FaceTime him via Messenger. And I needed to tell him the plan and teach him how to get hold of me via messenger. He had an iPad that he used for his game. I already downloaded the Facebook messenger app on his iPad.

I took him for dinner after I picked him up from school so I could tell him the plan while he was in a good mood. Back then, he loved the Asian Buffet place. I took him to the Buffet on SE and Stark. While we were eating a variety of foods, I said,

"BABA," (I call him BABA), "I want to ask you something." He couldn't wait.

He said, "What?"

I said,

"If your babysitter decides not to watch the kids anymore, including you, what do we have to do? Where do you want me to take you?" I was asking him as if he were responsible for himself.

He said,

"Bontu's house,"

I said,

"You know, Bontu has worked every day except Saturday and Sunday."

He thought for a second by putting his pointer finger on his lip. He said, "Uhmii. Then I can stay by myself. I guess."

I asked, "Are you sure you stay by yourself? You're not scared?"

He said, "What would I fear? Yes, I can stay by myself. I can watch TV and play with my iPad."

When I saw his confidence, I wanted to cry, but I couldn't do that in front of him and the public. His innocence was the thing that made me emotional.

I pretended I was happy about his response, but I also felt guilty to be seeking advice from this innocent child.

In my head, I said, "You already read my mind, brave kid."

We got home with full stomachs around 7:00 p.m. We played together wrestling and a staring contest. That's what we loved to do after dinner. It was then time to go to bed. He liked to tuck in. I read him some virtue of the Holy Book. We slept together. He loved head scratching. It soothed him, and he fell asleep quickly.

Before he fell asleep, I said,

"Baba, you know you are not going to go to the babysitter's home after a week or so. You will stay at home by yourself when I go to work."

The reason I was asking him again was to check whether he took it seriously or not.

He said,

"I know. I already told you; I can stay by myself. Why do you keep asking me?"

I said,

"I will give you a phone call. Then you will call me when you're scared or need something; I will come immediately. I don't go far."

I thought he was listening to me while I was talking, but he had already fallen asleep. I continued talking to him until I heard his snore. Then I kissed him on his cheek and laid down next to him, but I didn't want to sleep. I got up from bed and sat on the floor, then bowed on the ground on my head and started praying on the matter. This is the true thing I am sharing with you, folks.

I asked God to tell me if what I was doing right now was right. And I asked him to guide me in the right way. I asked him if leaving this little boy at home by himself was safe or not. I asked him again if I was going to be in trouble. And I asked him the solution to all my questions. And then, I got the answer!

Believe me; I got the answer right there before I picked up my head from the ground. It was something like assurance. Something like we will be safe and protected. Something like he never left us alone. I could feel that nothing bad would happen to us. I could feel the environment around me become calm and peaceful. I could sense the calmness throughout the room. I heard a sound like my mom's, saying to keep working hard, that I was covered, and my son was covered, too. The only thing I needed to do was trust. Trust God. No one would betray me. I weren't by myself. God was always with me. He is close to me. Never doubt it for a second. Never give up. Never complain. Never get fear. Fear is your worst enemy. Always be positive.

I didn't want to get up from that peaceful moment. But the message was over. Then, I slowly started hearing a sound in my area, like my son's snoring. After that, I felt so peaceful. I went to sleep.

Again, I saw the dream, and my dad repeated the same message. "Don't worry. Just trust your God and pray. You will overcome all these difficulties." It sounded like my father was talking to me. I didn't even think it was a dream until I woke up to use the bathroom.

I dropped Obama off at the school in the morning and left to drive an Uber. My son would stay at the afterschool program until I came and got him. I needed to stop driving around 3:30 or 4:00 because I didn't want to get stuck in traffic. On top of that, I didn't know where the riders would take me after those hours. The riders might take me far away. If that happened, I didn't have someone to pick Obama up for me. Those hours were rushing hours in Portland. I pick him up around 4:15 or 4:30 from his afterschool program.

We went home. While he was taking a shower, I cooked dinner. We ate. After that, I left for Uber around 5:30 or 6:00 p.m. for an hour and a half or two hours. That time was busy, especially at the airport. I came home at 8:00 or 8:30. I gave Obama a snack. While he was eating the snack, I took a shower; then, we immediately went to sleep. Every morning, I wake up at 3:00 a.m.

OF COURSE, UNDREAMED

In the morning, I left for Uber while he was sleeping. He didn't wake up until I came back home at around 6:30 or 7:00 a.m. When I got home, I woke him up and gave him breakfast. Our breakfast usually consisted of cereal, scrammed eggs, PB&J sometimes, or oatmeal with some fruit. Then, I dropped him at school and went back to Uber until his pickup time. This is my everyday business now.

When I left for Uber in the mornings, I didn't tell him. If I told him, I thought he might get worried or scared in the night and wake up. He might start worrying about me if he didn't see me around the house. That's why I left him sleeping, not to mention the fact that he was not a morning person.

When I left for Uber in the evening, I told him I was going to work. I told him to make sure he called me via messenger every twenty minutes or answered the call when I called him. At the same time, I warned him not to open the door to anyone, including me. When he called me, even if I had a rider, I would answer the call by first apologizing to the rider. Most of the time, it was me calling every twenty minutes. He was a good boy. He would always answer the call right away and confirm that he was ok.

Uber became my main job. I worked ten hours a day. I started living with Uber money. I was able to pay all my bills. I even started saving some extra money. My income from The Home Depot went straight to my savings account. I had never saved money since I came to America.

It was around Christmas time. One evening, I picked up one very drunk guy. It was obvious for most of the ride. When I picked him up, he asked me where I was from due to my accent.

He said,

"Your accent is different. Where are you from?"

I told him I was from Ethiopia.

He asked,

"Why did you leave your country?"

I replied,

"For a better life."

He said,

"Better life? Driving Uber is a better life for a woman like you? Driving in the middle of the night?"

I said,

"Yes, it is better for me." He didn't know my situation.

He said,

"Shame on you."

I was so shocked and scared when he said that. I didn't expect it. I thought he was going to feel bad for me.

OF COURSE, UNDREAMED

And he kept asking me unnecessary questions. It made me nervous and uncomfortable.

Still, he continued asking,

"How many children do you have?"

I told him two. I lied.

He said,

"How old are they?"

I answered,

"Thirteen and twelve years old."

He asked,

"Boys or girls?"

I said,

"Both are boys."

He said again,

"Shame on you."

I wanted to ask him why he was saying such a cruel thing to me, but I was scared.

"Why don't you teach them how to drive the car, then they will help you? You don't have to drive at night."

I said, "They are minors."

He said again, "Yes, they can drive. Shame on you. When I was fourteen years old, I helped my mom with a lot of things. You are not a strong mom, so you didn't teach your children how to help you. Shame on you."

I was getting nervous. I was very scared. I wanted to tell him that the way he was talking to me was making me uncomfortable, but I was scared. I was scared to death. I couldn't wait until he left my car. I wanted to tell him to leave my car immediately. But if I did, I was worried he might hurt me, so I was driving with fear. I imagined what would happen if I told him to leave my car. Still, I was driving towards his destination.

I think the ride was about ten minutes long, but it felt like ten hours to me. I stopped talking to him and raised the radio volume to pretend I didn't hear him or the questions he was asking.

Finally, I arrived at his destination. Before he got out of my car, he said, "Hold on, I have to give you something for your children as a Christmas gift."

He put his hand inside his pocket. I thought he was going to take out a gun from his pocket and shoot me in my head from behind. I wanted to get out of my car, but I didn't want to leave him in my car. I reminded myself that this was just a Christmas gift for my son. Still, I was shaking. I wanted to leave the car and run. But then, I realized he'd probably be able to catch up with me and get me. I prayed to God to save me. My heart was pounding. While I was taking my last breath, his hand came out of his pocket with a wallet—not with a gun. I breathed deeply.

He opened his wallet and took out a bill, which I couldn't differentiate between what the bill was because it was dark.

He said, "Here, buy your kiddos something for Christmas." Then, he handed me the money. I couldn't believe it. It felt like a dream. I took the money from him.

He struggled a lot to get out of my car. Finally, he managed it. Right after he closed my car door, I hit the gas pedal and disappeared from the area. After I went far from his location, I looked at the bill and saw that it was $100. It was crazy!

After that, I didn't take any more rides. I turned off my apps and headed toward home, and that night turned from a nightmare to a miracle.

When I went to ride Uber, I didn't tell my son that I was driving Uber. I was worried that he might worry and think too much if he knew what I was doing. He might worry that I would get in an accident. The only thing I would tell him was that I was going to work, and I'd be right back. "Don't forget to call or answer the call when I call you." That's it. I just told him that. Finally, one day, I told him I was an Uber driver when he turned eleven years old.

I left him with a snack, water, and his iPad—our communication machine. At the same time, I warned him not to get up from the couch. I warned him not to walk around the house except to go to the bathroom.

And I warned him not to turn the TV's volume up. He might not have heard my call if he had turned up the volume.

One day after we got home from school, it was time for me to go to Uber. I told him the same thing I always did. "Here is water, a snack, and here is your iPad. Hey, remember to call me or answer when I call you." Then I left.

I headed to the airport. I waited for the request in the backfield, where we waited for the ride. I waited for fifteen minutes; then I got a request from the airport. While I was heading to the airport, I called my son, but he didn't answer. Again, I called him before I picked up the rider. Obama didn't answer. Then, I arrived at the pickup location. After I picked up the rider, I asked the rider if it would be ok with him to make a quick emergency call. The rider was ok with that. I called again, but he didn't answer. When I started the trip, the rider was going to Hillsboro, which was forty minutes from the airport. When I accepted the request, I hoped the rider would not go that far. I was hoping Obama would answer the phone, so I kept calling him again and again, but he didn't answer. I started worrying. Meanwhile, I didn't want to tell the rider about my situation. How could I tell the stranger what was going on? I called again, but my son didn't answer. I wished I could drop off the rider halfway, but I was worried he might give me a bad rating and complain about it. My heartbeat was becoming fast.

I said, "Oh God! Help me with this. I trust you. Don't let any bad things happen to me. God, we already have an agreement. You promised me you wouldn't let me down."

I arrived at the rider's destination. I dropped him off right away and started driving home. The traffic on Highway 26 was horrible. Highway 26 was piled up to the Highway 217 exit. I had to find a faster route to be home as soon as possible. It was around 6:00 p.m. I exited Highway 26 and took the back road, Cornelius Road. I needed to sneak in every chance I got, I needed to drive over the speed limit, honk at the drivers who drove slowly, and cut them off whenever I got the chance.

Still, I was calling Obama, but he weren't answering. My situation was terrifying. I noticed that I was getting crazy. So, I needed to calm down. If anything had happened to him already, it was done, and I couldn't change it now. At the same time, I cursed myself for thinking that way. I was scared to deal with any consequences. I was scared. Again, I regretted thinking so negatively. I read some verses of the holy book, one that I had memorized. That made me calm down and focus. I kept reading and singing spiritual songs to divert my attention from thinking bad stuff. I hadn't heard my son's voice for an hour and a half.

Finally, I arrived home. I looked around while I was parking my car, but nothing had changed. I just ran upstairs without turning off the car. I couldn't finish running up the stairs because I was so weak, and my heart was beating so fast. I held the handrails to support me in walking fast. I got to the front door. Then, I reached the door, but I forgot the house key in the car. I wanted to call out his name, but at the same time, I didn't want to call his name because the neighbors might hear me. I didn't want the neighbors to know about my situation. So, I ran back down to the car to get the key. I couldn't find the key. I forgot where I put the key. I searched for the key inside my bag. I couldn't find it. I was in a rush, and I didn't have time to keep looking.

So, I needed to go upstairs again and knock on the door. I knew he would not open the door for me because I warned him not to open it even if it was me. I still had to try to knock on the door and tell him it was me. If he responded and I heard his voice, I would be ok. I rushed upstairs with very weak legs. I knocked on the door and called him, "BABA." He responded, "Yeah?"

OMG! I just fainted right there. I slipped on the ground and sat there for a while.

He was curious, and he called out, "Emma."

I responded, "Yes, I am here."

OF COURSE, UNDREAMED

He was waiting for me to open the door. I told him I lost the key. Then he opened the door for me. When I got inside, I asked him why he didn't answer my calls.

He said,

"Sorry, Emma, I forgot. I was watching TV." I saw that his iPad was on the ground. He hadn't seen it. Then, I forgot that I had never turned off the car engine. The car was running for about two hours. I saw my car's headlight when I went to bed through the window. My bedroom window was right above the parking lot.

I thanked God for everything and let the night pass.

One day, I remember taking a lady to Hood River City from the airport at around 9:30 p.m. I dropped Obama off with some friends that night because he didn't have school in the morning. It was around Christmas, and school was closed for winter break. I remember it was a solstice day which is December 21st—half of the year, and it was the longest and darkest day of the year. This lady was visiting her family for Christmas, as she told me. I had to drive her through Colombia Gorge. It was in the forest and dark. It was very dark. On top of that, there were no streetlights. The road was windy, too. It took me an hour to get there. I was ok when I was heading there because the lady was with me. But I was worried about the way back. I was so scared. If something happened, I was done. I didn't know what to do on such a night. I was so panicked. There were not many drivers on the road. I only saw some drivers after a while. Luckily, nothing happened to me, and I got home safely with God's help.

In the same week, one guy asked me to take him to Hood River City. It was around 6:00 p.m. The guy looked angry. He was saying bad things about his family.

He said,

"They want me to go there, but I don't want to go there." He even mentioned Radio Cub drivers and how much he doesn't like them. Then he asked me if I could take him there, that he would pay $100. Hell no! I weren't even happy about the way he talked about his family, let alone taking him there. How could I trust him and take him through that jungle? I didn't trust him. What would I do if he kidnapped me? I thanked him for the offer and refused to take him.

I said,

"No thanks, I don't want to go there. I have something to do here."

Then when he left my car, he said,

"Fuck you," and he slammed my door and left.

Still, I continued driving Uber. It was New Year's Eve. I liked driving on Christmas Eve and New Year's Eve in Portland. I make good money on those nights. Those nights I leave Obama with my friend Bontu. He would sleep there. Bontu worried about me when I went driving at night.

That day, I dropped Obama with Bontu and left for my business. I picked up one guy. He looked a little bit drunk and confused. He even called me Nancy when he got in my car.

I said,

"I am not Nancy."

He said,

"Sorry."

I didn't know what happened to him, but he started crying, cussing, and cussing, and crying. He occasionally said sorry. It was crazy. I was getting nervous about his situation. I kept my eyes on him through my rear-view mirror. He just threw his head down and kept cussing. I wanted to ask him what the matter was, but at the same time, I was scared. Luckily, he weren't going far. I dropped him at his destination and took off right away.

Then, I headed to the next rider's location. I picked up the rider, drove to the destination, then dropped him off. Most rides were peaceful.

It was around 10:30 p.m. when I picked up three big guys. They looked to be in their mid-twenties. They were drunk, too. I think they wanted to go home. Right away, they got in my car and started talking trash. I ignored them and focused on the road.

One of the guys who was sitting in the middle said,

"Her car is shaking," and the other two who were sitting right and left him laughed at what he said. They laughed very loud, and that made me uncomfortable. I could see what they were doing in the reflection of my mirror. It looked like they wanted to mess with me because I'm a Black woman and an immigrant. They started mocking me. It made me upset. I told them I was aware of what they were doing, and that I didn't like it. I asked them to stop. I added,

"If you don't stop mocking me now, I will drop you in the middle of the street. I'm not scared of you junk guys." They ignored me and kept mocking me. They mocked my accent. I was so upset. They thought it was fun.

Now, I needed to find a safe place to unload them from my car. If I told them to leave my car right away, they might retaliate against me. So, I needed to be wise, and I needed to control my emotions. I kept looking for a safe place and saw that the police were in my way. I completely ignored them. Then, I saw a police car parked in the distance on the side of the road. I slowed down and got close to the police car. I stopped my car right there.

They said,

OF COURSE, UNDREAMED

"What are you doing? Why are you stopping here?"

I said,

"You are trash people; I'm taking you home safely in the middle of the night, but you guys are not nice people. You guys are stupid. Drunk people and fat asses. You kept mocking me even when I asked you respectfully to stop it. You ignored me and kept making fun of me. You know I speak more than four languages. You only speak one language and try to make fun of someone who is way, way smarter than you. You don't appreciate the service. You are drunk and don't know where to go or what to do, and I am a Black immigrant woman taking you home safely. You don't deserve to be in my car. Get out of my car right now unless you want me to call a police officer. I am not comfortable driving you to your home. You guys are dangerous. "Get out of my car." I raised my voice to be in control. I don't want to be seen as a weak woman by them. "Get out of the car now!" I yelled at them and opened my door. I got out of the car and walked towards the police car.

When I walked towards him, the police officer saw me, came out of his car, and said, "What's the matter?"

I told him I was an Uber Driver and had three drunk guys in my car. I told him they were mean to me and mocked me since I picked them up. I continued telling the police that I didn't feel safe taking them home.

I told him I was scared they might hurt me, so I didn't want to drive them home. Even when I politely asked them to stop, they were not nice at all, and they kept doing it.

"Can you please take them out of my car?" I asked.

The police officer was a white guy. He walked towards my car and asked the guys what the problem was. They were still in my car.

They said, "Nothing."

He said, "What happened?"

Again, they said, "Nothing."

I said, "They were trying to hurt me."

They chimed in, "That is a lie."

I interrupted them and said, "I am not lying. They were mocking me the whole time. Plus, I have the right to refuse the service when I feel it is unsafe, and I can cancel it anytime. Officer, please tell them to leave my car." But the officer didn't take me seriously. He even tried to convince me to take them to their destination.

Finally, he said,

"You guys can come out if she doesn't want to take you."

They left my car, and I drove away. After that, I turned off the Uber app and went home. I saw the difference between the way the cop treated me and the way he treated the white guys in my car. He didn't even bother to ask what happened. When they told him I was lying, he believed them. He didn't raise his voice towards them and kindly asked them to leave my car.

Still, I was driving Uber. It was my job—the job I depended on. I pick different people. Some of them were very nice and humble. Some of them were very rude and grumpy. Some of them were very loud and crazy. Some of them were ignorant and arrogant. But most of the time, my riders were nice and ordinary people. I also noticed that young people between the ages of twenty-one to thirty were louder and crazy. They loved very loud music, especially when they were drunk.

One day I picked up this lady who was going to the airport. As usual, she asked me where I was from. I could see her arrogance. She didn't ask me in a mannered way. I replied to her that I was from Africa.

She said,

"It has been a long time since I took geography. Where is Africa located? Is Africa located in the Middle East?"

She thought that Africa was a country located in the Middle East. Can you imagine how stupid she must have been? She didn't even know Africa was a continent.

I told her,

"Africa is a continent like North America. It is not a country. It has fifty countries."

She said,

"Sorry." I could see her apology was fake. She continued,

"Is Africa still a jungle, or does it have some cities?"

I was so upset at her arrogance and ignorance. I wanted to respond to her, "Go back to the map and look," or, "Search on Google about Africa, then you will find more about it," but I didn't want to get a bad rating. I needed to be patient with her.

After I took a deep breath, I told her,

"Africa is a beautiful continent with fifty countries and beautiful cities like Johnsburg, Addis Ababa, Abuja, Legos, Nairobi, and some other big cities. Africa is the richest continent with natural resources, wild animals, and so on." Literarily, I was teaching her Africa 101. Finally, I told her to watch the National Geography channel to learn more about Africa. She felt her stupidity and ignorance, but she didn't want to apologize for being arrogant and ignorant.

I said in my head,

"You are a very stupid grown woman." After that, I didn't say anything to her, and she didn't, either. I think she was ashamed of herself when I outsmarted her. At the end of the ride, I dropped her at the airport, rated her one star, and commented that she was arrogant and not nice to the driver.

One night, one person requested a ride, but then five people came to get the ride. My car could fit only four people. When I told them I didn't have enough room, one of them said they would get in the trunk.

I said,

"OMG! You are kidding me; you guys are crazy. I won't take you in my trunk. Bye!" Then I canceled the request and mentioned the reason for cancelation—too many riders.

When you drive during the night, you will encounter different people with different attitudes, especially those who are celebrating their twenty-first birthday. They become drunk easily and become emotional quickly. I think the reason for that was that they were not used to so much alcohol in their systems.

One night, this beautiful girl with a tiara on her head came towards me with her three friends to ask if I could take them to their homes. I told her she needed to request a ride through Uber; then, I could take her home.

She said,

"I don't want to request Uber; Uber will charge me extra if in case someone gets sick and vomits in the car."

I said,

"Umhi, you are trying to be smart. You mess up my car; then you leave me with your mess. You don't want to pay the cleaning cost when you mess up somebody's car." Uber charges $250 if someone throws up in the driver's car. She wanted to save money. In addition, how could I trust her if she was going to pay me in cash? I said, "Good luck with your smart thinking," and I left.

Right away, before I even made a turn, one of them requested Uber. I knew that they were the ones who requested it because the app showed me the same place. I turned back to the pickup location, and I picked them up. One got in the front seat, and the rest sat in the back. They didn't recognize me as the person they were just talking to five minutes ago because they were drunk and tired. It was around 1:30 a.m. Two of them were going to the same place. The other two were going to a different location. After I dropped two of them in two different locations, the one with the tiara started vomiting in my car. I was so upset. She could have asked me to stop the car. She could have gotten out and vomited on the ground. Believe me; it was a mess.

Her friend said,

"Sorry, she just turned twenty-one, that is why she is drunk. She is not used to alcohol. I will clean it for you, believe me." She took her little jacket out and threw it on the floor where her friend's vomit was. She wiped it with her jacket. When I dropped them off, she said,

"I will be right back; I will bring some spray and a paper towel, and I will clean it for you."

I said,

"Never mind," and I took a photo of the vomit and sent it to Uber customer service. After I dropped them, I put all four windows down and headed home. My car was so smelly. I hated that. Uber sent the rider a $250 cleaning fee.

Another night, four boys came towards me to get a ride. They asked me how to request an Uber. I showed them. Right away, their request came to me. I picked them up, and they were going to Lewis and Clark College. They were coming from a concert. The person who was sitting in the front seat next to me smelled horrible. He smelled like water never touched his body. His body smelled like a skank. The smell that came from his armpit struck my nose. I was very sensitive to any smells by my nature. I started sneezing right away. I kept sneezing and sneezing. At the same time, I wanted to throw up. Struggling through my feelings, I dropped them off. I threw up right when they left my car. My nose and throat started hurting me. Due to that I was sick for two weeks and couldn't do Uber.

I still remember that day. It was January 10th, 2017. It snowed very badly for the first time since

1943. The city of Portland was not prepared for these two to three feet of snow. When it snowed in Portland, everything shut down—no work, no school, no flights, and nothing moved around. The road becomes icy and slippery. On top of that, the drivers in Portland didn't know how to drive in snowy weather on an icy road. Everyone was stuck on the road or at home. I didn't drive for five days. Some people made a lot of money, as I heard from friends. Uber gave a very good surge price. Usually, the ride from downtown Portland to the airport was between $14 and $16. On those snowy days, it became $100. One of my friends told me that he made $1000 in a day. It was just in one day he made that money. He told me I should go out and do Uber in the snow.

He said,

"You should do it. It is nice money. The main road and the freeways are already cleaned up, and the rest of the snow is melted."

I said, "Ok, I will do it tomorrow."

This time, my son was at home. He didn't have school due to the severe weather. I left him while he was watching TV. When I came out of my apartment after five days, a lot of snow was still on the ground outside. It had already turned to ice. Some neighbors tried to clean their driveways. I saw one guy coming out from the parking lot next to me. I followed him. His car was a pickup truck. He cleaned up the path for me. I followed him. Coming out of the apartment weren't so bad. After driving out of our alley, the neighborhood roads were still icy and had a lot of snow. I need to be more conscious. I have some experience driving in snow from Iowa. That helped me understand how to control my car. Right away, I saw people had chained up their tires, and some had traction tires. Just before I went far, Uber gave me one ride. I accepted it. It weren't far from me.

Now, I am heading towards the rider to pick them up on E Burnside and 146th Ave. My car started sliding side to side, but I didn't hit either the brake or the gas. I just had to be gentle. I needed to hold the steering wheel tight. I needed to be calm and relaxed. I needed to avoid panicking whenever the car slides. I kept my attention on the road, and I was very focused. When I got to Burnside, I needed to turn left. While I was turning to the left, my car's front tires got stuck on the train track. I tried to move out of it by hitting the gas, but the tire kept spinning. I put it in reverse, but it was still spinning. The car stopped going forward and backward. One of the front tires got stuck on the train track. I knew the train would come any minute. Now, I was getting panicked. If the train came and didn't see my car, my car would be damaged badly. The time was running out fast, I needed to do something.

I saw two drivers coming from East Burnside. They were heading west. I got out of my car and screamed, "Help, Help, please! I am stuck." They jumped out of their car right away and pushed my car forward. My car was free, no longer stuck on the train track. I was lucky to have seen those drivers. I saw the train coming minutes after they pushed my car off the track. I was saved that day, too.

A week after the big snow, I woke up early in the morning to drive Uber. It was around 3:30 a.m. Most of the ice on the road had melted. Still, there was some snow on the ground, especially in the hilly areas. I left Obama at home while he was sleeping. His school had resumed the normal schedule, so I needed to go back home to pick him up and drop him off at school on time. I started my car and headed toward downtown Portland.

While I was on I-84, I got a request on SE and Franklin. I exited the freeway and then headed to the riders, who were husband and wife. When I went to their house, the GPS took me on a less snowy road. After I picked them up, the husband told me to go a different way that he thought would be faster. The road he took me on was a little bit hilly. My car didn't do a good job on hills in the snow. Then, right as I turned to the road, he preferred the car started sliding down the hill. I hit the gas, but the car kept sliding. They were going to the airport, and the husband was getting frustrated. I did my best, but the car couldn't move forward; instead, it continued to slide downhill. I could see that my car was getting close to a parked car. I didn't want to crash into that car. Still, the car was getting close to hitting the other car, which was parked on the street. While I was struggling with the situation, the husband left my car to get his truck, and he left his wife with me in the car. He came back with his truck, and they unloaded their luggage and left me in that situation. Now, the time was 4:20 a.m. What could I do? I was stuck.

I called my friend Midhaksa. I knew he woke up early to drive like me. I called him around 5:00 a.m. He answered the phone.

He said,

"Are you ok? You never call this early in the morning."

I said,

"Yes, I am ok, but my car is stuck on the road."

I told him the story and I told him where I was. One guy was walking up and down the street. I feared him. He was on the other side of the road. Then, Midhakasa arrived around 5:30 a.m. We started pushing my car down the street. The guy who was walking around came to help. Finally, we were able to move my car out of the snow and turn the front tire downhill. The car started moving downhill. Then, I got in the car and started driving slowly down the street. All in all, the situation took me two hours. I was cold and shivering. It was twenty-eight degrees Fahrenheit. I drove home directly. I was saved that day too!

Chapter Eight

Accident and Its Consequences

On Wednesday, February 8th, 2017, I dropped my son off at school at around 8:10 a.m. Then, I opened the Uber app. The request came right away. It was on 82nd Street and SE Washington. I was on Stark Street, heading west. I needed to turn left on the 82nd to go to the pick-up location. I did. The light in front of me on Washington Street was red—as people around the area told me later, but I didn't see it. I was busy thinking about my family back home. I missed them a lot. I weren't even aware of the traffic around me. I thought the traffic light ahead of me was green. I just went through the light, and I crashed into the car heading east. I damaged the driver's door badly. And my car kept sliding, and I hit another car heading north that was waiting for the green light, and finally, my car stopped. My car was damaged badly in the front. The driver of the first car I hit couldn't come out of his car because his door was damaged badly. Anyhow, he managed to come out. Luckily, he weren't injured. I was so traumatized by the situation. My whole body was shaking.

He came towards me and said, "Are you ok?"

I said I was ok, even though I weren't.

One lady who was behind the guy that I hit came and said,

"I have a camera that recorded the traffic light. If you need it, I will give you." She took his number and told him to contact her if he needed to. He took my insurance information and gave me his, too. And the other driver that my car slid into and hit took my insurance info and left. My car was damaged badly in the front, and it was leaking fluids. I couldn't drive it or move it. Everybody left me there. I was by myself. I was so stressed out.

Again, I called Midhaksa—who had quickly become my rescue guy. I told him I got into an accident. I told him where I was. He was close. He came right away. He told me I needed to tow the car. At the same time, he contacted the collision repair center he knew about. That collision center was the Kesey Collision Repairer Center. They sent me the tow track. We towed the car to the center. I agreed to fix my car with them. They told me they would inspect the damage and they would send me the estimate to fix it if it weren't totaled.

Here go! Another challenge and difficulty. Again! No car to drive Uber, then no income. How could I pay my bills? If the guy didn't fix my car as soon as possible, what was I going to do? That frustrated me. I asked him how long it would take to fix my car or total it.

He said,

"The car is fixable, but I need time to get the parts. I already have a lot of cars ahead of you. Give me time."

If I went through my insurance, I'd have to pay the deductible first, which was $1,000. I needed to pay out of pocket. On top of that, I didn't know how long it was going to take them to fix my car. On the other hand, Kasey didn't ask for a deductible. I had a little money that I saved, but I didn't want to risk that money. The bills would come soon too. Now, I was getting stressed out and depressed.

Still, I needed to find a solution to my situation. I needed to figure out how to not fall behind in my bills. One thing came to mind. Last time when I was in the backfield waiting for an airport request, I saw a couple of Russian women bringing something for snacks for taxis, Uber, Lyft, and some van drivers. They made a little pocket money. I knew many drives there; thus, I could make some snacks and coffee, and they would buy it from me. That would help me with some bills. I needed to do that. I needed to make snacks, coffee, and tea and start selling to Uber, Lyft, and taxi drivers. I hoped that they would support me by buying from me. So, right away I started making pastries, samosas, coffee, and tea in the morning and afternoon. I did it for a month and a half. I made some money and covered my bills by adding the Home Depot income. I still worked at the Home Depot on Saturday and Sunday. Finally, my car was ready to pick me up, and I passed through a difficult time.

Again, I needed to go back to driving Uber because I didn't have a choice. For a couple of months after the accident, I was traumatized, and I panicked when the cars passed by me or close to me.

Now, I could see where my weakness was and what I needed to do to get over it. Whenever something unexpected happened, I became stressed and depressed. Depression was already there. I decided to look for someone who could help me at least with bills. I liked having someone that I could lean on and depend on during difficult times. In the first place, I might not have difficulties if I had someone next to me. I needed to start moving on. Working hard by myself was exhausting. I had already developed depression in Phoenix. I didn't want to continue in the same situation. More importantly, before I moved on with this idea, I needed to tell my son that I wanted to find someone who could help me. I didn't want to make my son uncomfortable with my idea, and first, I needed to make sure he would be okay with it.

I said to him, "Baba, I am tired of running here and there, up and down, by myself, so are you going to be mad at me if I start dating someone who can help both of us?"

Obama was happy. He said, "Sure Emma, you need someone who can help you, and I need a father figure in my life too, like my friends." I cried after hearing his very wise advice. I was so happy that my little one was a very understanding person.

I said,

"Are you sure, Baba? You won't get jealous when I get a husband?"

He said,

"No, I want you to be happy, Emma. I want you to be healthy. I don't want to see you tired every day."

After I got permission from him, I needed to seek advice from a couple of people. My brother Ibro is back home, and Bontu is. Bontu was happy and supportive of my idea.

She said,

OF COURSE, UNDREAMED

"I will be happy for you if you find the right one." At the same time, I didn't want to tell my mom, because I felt telling her would be inappropriate.

I told her that I didn't have a husband right now, but I would start looking for one. She told me to pray for it and the right person will come in the will of God. I told my brother Ibro the same thing. He asked me if I already had someone in mind. I told him I didn't.

He said,

"Pray about it, and I will pray for you too."

He continued,

"Let's open our hearts for good things and it will happen. I will tell our dad to pray   for you too."

I said "OK'. After that, the network was bad, and we didn't talk.

I was still driving Uber. One day, I gave a ride to a family who came from Oman, Jordan. A mom, daughter, and son. I picked them up from the airport. They were heading to Corvallis. The mom's other son was a student at Oregon State University. They came to visit him. Driving from Portland to Corvallis takes about an hour and thirty minutes. The lady was nervous about me driving. As her daughter told me, women don't drive taxis in their country. While we were on the way to Corvallis, the mom got worried that I might fall asleep on the way. So, she insisted that her daughter sit next to me and talk to me so I wouldn't fall asleep.

I let my daughter sit next to me. The mom only spoke Arabic. The daughter was the one who could speak English. I asked the daughter why her mom was worried. The daughter replied, "She thinks you might fall asleep while you are driving. She wants me to talk to you and keep you awake."

I laughed and said, "This is my professional job. Tell your mom not to worry." In contrast, she is the one who fell asleep while we were on the road. I dropped them off and came back home directly.

Another time, this old lady I picked up from a restaurant asked me where I was from.

I told her I was from Ethiopia.

She said,

"I heard many things about Ethiopia. And I read a book about Ethiopia. It is rich in history and resources. I read about Arc of Covenant in some magazines found in Ethiopia. Is it true that still Ethiopia has it today? Is it true or it is a myth?"

I told her that I don't practice that religion, but I believed it is still there in the northern part of Ethiopia church called Axum Tsion. Axum Tsion is the place that the Arc Covenant is still at as religious people claim. It is very secure and protected. Nobody knows where the Arc itself locate except a few priests. That is the treasure of the country.

She said,

"That is interesting."

We talked about different topics. Finally, we got to the destination. While she was leaving my car, she gave me a $50 tip. Nice lady!

In my experience, older people know about the world more than young people. They are very interested to know about you and your country. They know history better than younger folks.

Another day, I picked up two students from the airport who were coming from Asia on winter break. They were going to Astoria. I picked them up around 8:30 p.m. Driving west was horrible at that time because it got dark early. It was very dark. Highway 26 became very narrow and there were a lot of forests too. Most of the time, there was no phone or GPS signal. I kept driving. They didn't speak English, so I couldn't have a conversation with them. I drove for an hour and a half. Then we arrived at the destination—a college. College was uphill. You needed to have a passcode to enter the college gate. They didn't have the passcode. We couldn't communicate due to the language barrier. I didn't know what to do. I couldn't leave them there in the jungle, but at the same time, I wanted to go home before midnight. If I got stuck on the road, it would be a disaster for me. It was already 10:00 p.m. I started praying for a miracle. The girls were panicking.

After thirty minutes, a car came from inside the college. The gate opened when the car approached. After the car left, I rushed and entered the gate before it closed on me. I drove five minutes to drop them off after I entered the college gate. Imagine if I left them there, what would happen to those girls? After I dropped them off, I put on my bright light and tried not to panic. I opened some verses of the holy book and listened to them while I was driving back as fast as I could. I got home at midnight.

By driving Uber, I went to many places in Oregon. I went to Eugene, Corvallis, Selam, Canby, Sandy, Estacada, Boring, Astoria, McMinnville, and even Washington State, even the far place called Chinook.

One morning, I dropped Obama off at the school and opened the app right away. But I couldn't get the request where I was, so I decided to go close to the downtown area. While I was heading to the downtown area, I got one request. When I accepted it, it said it would be a long ride, forty-five minutes or more. I was happy. You make better money from long rides, but on the way back, most of the time, you don't get a ride. I got to the pick-up place. The lady who requested the ride came and said, "I will tip you well if you take this guy home."

But I was expecting her to be my ride. Still, I said, "Ok. thanks."

The guy came right away. He got in my car. Then he started telling me that she was his boss and fired him.

He said,

"Here is his workplace. But my home is in Chinook, Washington. I drive the company's car, mine is at home, where you are taking me now."

I said,

"Ok." Other than that, I didn't have anything to say. At the same time, I was scared to take him that far. I had never been there. I tried not to show my fear to the guy. After two hours of driving, I got there and dropped him off, then hit my gas and left.

After some time, my brother Ibro called me to check on me and ask me if I was still looking for someone. I told him I was still open and looking for someone. He told me that if I was ok with it, he would hook me up with someone that he'd known for a long time. He was just giving me his opinion; it would be me who would accept or reject it. At the time, I was looking for someone who lived in the US, but I couldn't find one who would accept me with my son. If I found one, I would be ready to move forward. I needed to find someone who would take care of my son like his own child. I didn't want to bring someone into our lives that my son weren't going to approve of and would not be happy with him. All this suffering was for him. I preferred to stay a single mom for my whole life instead of bringing someone that couldn't get along with my son. I didn't want to make a mistake.

Before he told me, Ibro started talking to his long-time friend about me. His friend's name was Aman Tuke. Aman was back home in Ethiopia. Ibro told him everything about me, as he told me later. If Aman wanted to, he could hook him up with me. He gave Aman time to think about it. After a bit, Aman told Ibro that he weren't in a relationship, but Aman weren't sure if I would say yes or no. Ibro and Aman had known each other since the eighth grade. Ibro got consent from Aman to proceed, but he weren't sure if I would accept Aman either.

Some other time, Ibro called me, and we talked about family and some other stuff. In the middle of our conversation, he said,

"Would you mind if I hooked you up with someone?"

I asked,

"What kind of person?"

He said,

"He is a very good guy, and do you remember I told you last time about him? He is a friend of mine, and I have known him for a long time."

I said,

"How much do you trust him?"

He said,

"Two thousand percent."

Then I said, "Ok."

He said,

"Ok, thanks. By the way, are you ok if I give him your number? Then he can contact you."

I said,

"Ok, but that is rushed. I need to think about it, so give me a time before you give him my number."

Ibro said, "Ok."

Months passed. Again, another day, Ibro texted me to ask what I was thinking about the matter. I told him I weren't confident yet to say yes. Because I didn't know that person. I needed to learn more about him. And from nowhere, I was getting mad and questioning Ibro, "Who is this person? Why you are very serious about him?" I don't think I was stable with my thinking. My emotions kept swinging. Ultimately, I didn't want to decide before I knew the person very well.

Ibro noticed I was very hesitant to decide. So, he didn't want to push me. I think he also told my dad about the matter.

One day, when I called my dad to say hi, my dad started speaking strongly. He sounded like he was very series. He said,

"I am aware of your situation and struggle; I know you are sacrificing for your son. I don't want to force you, but I just want to give you a piece of advice as a dad. Just take your time and think about it. You need to change your life."

I told my dad that I didn't trust people based on my previous relationship. My dad left me with the choice that if I wanted to get help, they could help me with what they could. If not, I could keep struggling until my son becomes capable of helping himself and me.

My dad asked the same question as Ibro did if I had someone in mind in America. I told him as I didn't. At the same time, I needed to listen and respect my dad's advice. I knew my dad worried about me too.
After I thought about it for a couple of months, I told Ibro I was ready to move on. Ibro was happy about it when I told him. He said,

"Finally. I will hook you up with Aman, my best friend for a long time."

I said,

"Ok. But I will talk to your friend with pre-conditions."
So, I proceeded to tell Ibro the criteria I needed from his friend Aman.

OF COURSE, UNDREAMED

First, I didn't want a person who wanted to take advantage of me to come to the US because America was the country everyone wanted to be in.

Second, I wanted someone who respected me and my son. My son was the most important person to me.

Third, I wanted a person who was educated, or at least completed the twelfth grade, and had some common sense. I wanted someone flexible and adapted to change quickly.

Fourth, I wanted someone who was not in any relationship right now.

Fifth, I wanted someone who valued relationships and family.

Finally, I wanted someone who liked to work hard and who was progressive.

Ibro assured me that Aman was the perfect fit and could fulfill all the requirements. It was true that is Amen Tura—he is now my current husband!

Then I assured Ibro that he could give him my number.

After a couple of weeks, Aman starts calling me. I asked Aman before we initiated any conversation to tell me everything without hiding the truth. I asked him how he felt about me having a child. I asked him if he was ready to accept me with my weakness and strengths for the entire of his life. He replied that he was telling the truth and that he already knew everything about me. He told me that my brother, Ibro, had already told him everything about me, and he was ready to accept me. I liked his honesty, calmness, and how he lowered his voice when he spoke to me. I started liking him the more we talked. He weren't a very rushed person. Then, we started calling each other every day. Finally, we agreed to move on and continue the relationship.

Having a long-distance relationship was awful and challenging. Seriously, I hated the long-distance relationship. We FaceTime each other every day at certain times. We used Messenger for chatting. Sometimes we used WhatsApp and Viber to call each other. As I said earlier, the more we talked, the more I liked him, but I couldn't fall in love. The best thing about Aman was that he always left me with a choice—he never rushed me or forced me into anything. We kept up our communication for months. Finally, I decided to go to Ethiopia and marry him.

I told him about my decision, and he was so happy. He then surprised me by sending gifts overseas.

Then we set the day I would go to Ethiopia and the date for our wedding day. This would be my first time going back to Ethiopia since I came to the United States.

Now, I needed to work hard to save money for the trip. I needed to have money for the flight for both me and Obama, and I needed to have some extra pocket money. I needed to drive more hours with Uber. I still had my Home Depot job, but I needed to extend my driving time longer, like twelve hours of driving a day.

One day, I left to drive for Uber at around 3:30 a.m. I did that because there were always more airport rides at that time. I could make forty to fifty dollars easily. After I dropped someone off at the airport, I decided to go home because it was time for Obama to go to school. I turned off Uber and headed home.

When I arrived home, I saw an Emergency Ambulance parked in my parking spot. I was shocked. I was about to faint. "What happened? Why is EMR Ambulance in my spot? What happened to my son? Who called EMR on him." He didn't have a phone. I checked on him when I left, and he was ok—he was sleeping. I wondered, what happened in those hours? My heart was beating fast. I was struggling with all the questions that I did not have the answers to. I didn't even know what to do or say if something happened to my son. How was I going to face this? It was a terrifying situation. I was scared to leave my car, but at the same time, I wanted to rush to see my son know what happened to him. In this internal conflict, I wasted about five minutes. Finally, I told myself to face the truth and go inside the apartment, but my legs were weak. I had no energy. I tried to get out of the car. My legs were weak, and I couldn't stand on the ground. And walking upstairs was becoming difficult, and I felt like I was climbing up a mountain.

When I got to the apartment, I reached for the door and tried to open it. The door was locked. I said, "Why is the door locked?" Then, I put my ear to the door to listen for any voices, but I couldn't hear anything. I decided to open the door. I dumped everything inside my purse on the ground to search for the key. Then, I found the key and carefully opened the door. And guess what?

Nobody was at home.

Obama was sleeping deeply. I figured out later that the ambulance had been called for an emergency by a neighbor. I still didn't understand why they parked in my spot, but maybe that was just accidental.

I continued to drive Uber. I got to know some people from my country at the airport waiting area called the backfield. A few of them asked me where my son was when I went to work. I told them that I had left him at home. I remember one very nice guy who once summoned me from the crowd and told me not to tell anyone that I had left my son by himself. People might report me. He advised me not to leave him alone in case something happened because it would be very bad for me. Then, he gave me fifty bucks and said, "Please go home now." He frustrated me. I was scared and left for home right away. Whatever he said was repeated in my brain. When I got home, Obama was watching TV.

The trip to Ethiopia was getting closer. I needed to have money for shopping, the plane ticket, family, and pocket change. So, doing Uber was more necessary than ever. At the same time, I kept shopping around for a cheaper plane ticket. Finally, I found a cheaper ticket that left from Toronto, Canada. I booked it right away. It was cheaper than flying from the US cities. My flight was on July 13th, 2017.

I couldn't wait until the day of my flight. I missed everything. Moreover, I missed my mom, my dad, my brothers, and my sisters, and, of course, I was excited to be with Aman. I couldn't wait to see him. I missed the place where I grew up and missed my childhood friends. My memory took me back to my childhood when I used to go to play with friends. I remembered who I played with, what we used to play, and the school we attended.

We had already set our wedding day. It would be on July 23rd, 2017, at Shashamane, south of the Capital city of Addis Ababa. I bought my bridal and groomed clothes from the US for Aman and Obama. I told Aman that I didn't want a big wedding ceremony. I wanted it to be very simple with a few people. Aman agreed and arranged it that way.

Chapter Nine

Visit to Ethiopia

On Saturday, July 13th, 2017, Obama and I took a flight from PDX to Toronto, Canada. We had a one-day layover in Toronto. We stayed at a hotel that night and caught the flight from there the next day. The flight was thirteen hours long from Toronto to Addis Ababa, Ethiopia. To pass the time, we slept, watched movies, and talked about our excitement about going back to Ethiopia after six years. Thirteen hours passed like that. Obama watched more movies than me. To be honest, I couldn't fall asleep because of the excitement.

We arrived at Bole International Airport around 7:00 a.m. local time. The passenger assistance people assisted us with finding and carrying our luggage. To be frank, it would have been difficult without them to find the luggage in the hustle environment.

When we exited the terminal, I saw my mom from afar. I pointed towards her to show Obama where it was. My mom, four of my brothers, three of my sisters, Aman, and a couple of neighbors were waiting for us outside of the terminal. We found each other. Obama couldn't recognize anyone except Aman, whom he FaceTime a couple of times. For the first time, I saw Aman in person. Of course, we had seen each other through FaceTime, but this was our first time meeting in person. I thought he was a good-looking guy—tall and dark brown. I liked his color.

We got into the rental car. My mom and some of my siblings lived in Addis Ababa. We arrived home after thirty minutes of driving. By now, me and Obama were so tired. We traveled for forty-eight hours. My mom wanted us to eat, but we couldn't because we were so tired. On top of that, our sleeping pattern was messed up. We tried a little bit of food and went to sleep right away. I couldn't even talk to Aman.

When I woke up, it was already nighttime there. Everybody went to sleep except my mom. My mom gave us her room to sleep in. Obama and I slept there. Aman and my brothers slept on the sofa and on the ground in the living room. My mom and my sisters slept in another room.

After I woke up, I couldn't go back to sleep. I was shy because my mom was there, so I didn't want to talk to Aman in private until we legally got married. My mom heard me when I went to the bathroom, and she came to my room after I came from the bathroom. She was very happy to see me again. Sometimes when I got stressed out in the US, I called her and talked to her in my times of difficulty. She was always worried about me. Here prayers kept me safe. Seeing me was a miracle for her. She didn't think she was going to see me anytime soon due to my financial difficulties. We talked almost for the whole night. She didn't sleep at all.

Aman and Ibro left on the third day to arrange things for our wedding. Our wedding was in Shashamane, south of Addis Ababa. They needed to make sure everything was organized and ready for the day.

My wedding was in ten days. I did a little shopping before I took off to Shashamane. When there were three days left until the wedding, I left Addis Ababa with my sisters and my mom. The wedding was arranged at the Rift Valley Hotel. I had brothers and sisters who live in Shashamane too. I stayed in one of my sister's houses until the wedding day.

Finally, it was the day I had been waiting for—my wedding day. The day I had dreamed about, that I was so thrilled about. The day I would finally stop living as a single mom. It was so exciting; I am getting nervous about it.

The wedding ceremony was in the Rift Valley Hotel. Fifty people attended the ceremony. My son Obama was so happy for me. He came between the crowd and kissed and said,

"Congratulations, Emma! I am happy for you." When he said that, tears just started dripping from my eyes. I cried. Tears of joy flowed down my cheeks, and my makeup got messed up. I hugged him and kissed him and made him sit next to me on my crown chair. What a blessing it was! I finally became legally married.

After the ceremony was over, Aman and I stayed at the hotel, while Obama and all my family left for Addis Ababa. I cried again when Obama left. We had never once been separated since he was born. Before they took him, I called him and told him I would come to Addis tomorrow. I told him not to worry about me. He said,

"Ok, ok."

We stayed in Ethiopia for a month and a half. Obama and I came back to the US in September of 2017, and we left Aman behind.

Now, I need to go back to my driving job. The Home Depot position was taken by someone when I was away. They told me to reapply again as a new employee. I gave them a leave of absence notice, so I didn't understand why they wouldn't just take me back.

So, I needed to focus on Uber. It would be my only income now that I could depend on. The bad thing was that I was broke—I didn't have money. I needed to work hard. I needed money to cover all my bills and file a paper for Aman to come to the US. I needed to do it right away. The process might take longer if I didn't do it immediately. The process of immigration can be lengthy.

I started driving on Saturdays and Sundays, and I was making better money than I did on the weekdays. When I drove on Friday nights and the full days on Saturdays and Sundays, I made good money. I made around $600 to $700, which was more than I made on the weekdays.

Obama still babysat himself. He was more responsible since we came back from Ethiopia. He called me every twenty minutes when I left for driving. Sometimes, I would take him to Bontu's house if I needed to drive overnight.

Now, things were finally getting better. I was making better money and I already filed the immigration paperwork for Aman. On top of that, I invited my mom to come to the US too. the US Embassy in Ethiopia denied her visa the first time. I reapplied for her visa again and they gave it to her the second time. I paid $640 total for her visa. They gave her a temporary visitor's visa called B1/B2.

OF COURSE, UNDREAMED

My mom came to the US in November of 2017.

I was relieved. With my mom around, I didn't have to worry about Obama staying by himself. Aman's paperwork was on the right track, too. It had been about six months since I filed it. Now, it was in the Visa Center. It was so accelerated for me. Some people's cases could take up to a year or more to be in a visa center.

Now, I could drive Uber any time if I wanted to. I could drive twelve-hour shifts, day, and night. I drove twelve-hour shifts, especially on Fridays, Saturdays, and Sundays. Sometimes, Uber automatically closed the app on me when I reached twelve hours limit. While I worked, my mom took care of me and Obama. She cooked, cleaned, walked Obama to the bus, and walked him home after school. She became my superhero.

One day, it was New Year's Eve. I liked driving on that holiday in Portland. I got a request immediately. I drove to the location. The new year ball had already dropped. It was the time people were getting ready to go home. A father and son approached my car. I greeted them they got in. When I started the trip, it said the destination was in McMinnville. It was an hour and thirty-minute drive. I asked them to make sure they had put in the right destination.

They said,

"We're going to McMinnville."

I said, "What?"

They said,

"Yes, we are going there. We understand it is very far for you. You might be too scared to drive that far at night. If you want, you can cancel the trip."

The fair was $150. I didn't want to lose it. At the same time, I didn't want to drive that far in the middle of the night. Even on a normal day, it's not enjoyable to drive there. It's not a very diversified city. Trust me, I heard a lot about that city.

They were still in my car. I was confronted with my decision to take them. Finally, I decided to take them because I trusted God, so nothing bad would happen to me.

They said,

"What did you decide?"

I said,

"It is okay, let's go."

The dad said,

"I don't blame you if you cancel the ride."

I repeated,

"It is okay. Let's go."

They put their seatbelts on, and I started driving.

We had a nice conversation on the way there. They made me laugh. They appreciated my willingness to take them so far, and they appreciated my strengths.

When we got close to the destination, the son offered to come back to Portland with me for my safety.

He said,

"The road is so empty; we don't want you to be by yourself. In case anything happens, we don't want you to be there by yourself. People are not nice in here."

I said,

"I appreciate your kindness and offer, but don't worry, I will be fine. God is always with me." To be honest, I appreciate his kindness, but at the same time, I didn't trust him, either. I thought he might do something to me. If someone were to try to attack me from a distance, I could hit my gas and drive quickly until I escape. But if someone dangerous is already in my car, how would I escape?

I knew the guy was trying to help me or protect me, but my heart didn't trust him. On the other hand, if he took me back to Portland, who would take him back to McMinnville? I didn't want him to get charged again.

Finally, I arrived at my destination. The dad gave $50, and the son gave $30 as a tip. Altogether, they tipped me $80. I thanked them for their kindness and tip, and I hit the gas. I drove as fast as I could, and I arrived in downtown Portland at 2:00 a.m. I didn't want to go home right away. I wanted to do the morning airport rides. So, I just shut off the app for some time to take a break. Then, I opened it around 3:00 a.m. Right away, I got a request from the waterfront Marriot Hotel.

They were two guys who had two babies with them. I thought the babies' moms must have been with them too. After one of the guys arranged the car seat and the babies in my car, he said, "Let's go."

I asked,

"What about the mom?"

He said,

"No Mom. They are surrogate children. I and my husband will raise them. They are twins."

The other guy took another Uber because they had too much luggage with them.

The guy who was in my car looked so panicked with the babies. I could tell that he didn't have experience. He even had a hard time with the car seat. I had to help him. I wanted to ask him about the surrogate mom. I didn't have any knowledge about that. At the same time, I didn't want to make him uncomfortable. So, I needed to be careful. After I noticed he was seated and became calm, I asked him where the surrogate mom was from.

He said,

OF COURSE, UNDREAMED

"The surrogate mom is here in Selam, the babies were born a month ago. We got the egg from Ukraine, and the sperm is belonging to my husband. After fertilization, we found one lady in Selam, and she was our surrogate mom. That's it."

I continued to ask more questions because the subject was very interesting to me.

I said,

"First of all, how did you find the lady who gave you the egg? Second, how did you find the surrogate mom? And lastly, how much did it cost you?"

He seemed annoyed at my questions and said,

"Everything is on the internet."

He just shut me off there. After that, I didn't ask more questions. After I dropped him off, I shut down my app and went home because I was so tired.

After a while, I heard about the same topic on the radio about the children who were born from surrogate moms and stranded in Nepal when an earthquake hit in 2015. Those children were in hospital on the day of the earthquake. Some of them got delivered on the same day. It was a terrifying situation. Their family couldn't go there to get them. As I heard on the radio, many surrogate children have died in hospitals. It was a lot of mess.

Forget about surrogate moms, let's turn our attention to my experience. It is my nature to try different things. One day, when I was looking at Facebook, I saw a sponsored ad that said, "Do you want to start a business on Amazon as a third-party seller?" The ad caught my attention, and I started searching for the topic. I learned about what it means to be a third-party seller on Amazon. But I need more information about how to do that. I referred to the ads. This company called Sellers Play Book wanted to give training on how to be a third-party seller on Amazon. They offered training for one day at the Sheraton Hotel near the airport. I was required to sign up for the training. It said that the training was free for one day. I signed up for the training, which was on January 8th, 2018.

I attended the training. A lot of people were in attendance too. The training was given by a few different people. After the training was over, they required us to sign up for another training course that would help us to be a successful third-party seller. The first day of training weren't enough to give more information and it's overwhelming too. My interest in the business was high, so I didn't hesitate to sign up for another training. To sign up for the second training, you needed to pay $250. I paid right on the spot. They gave me a receipt and training location, which was at the Double Tree by Hilton on January 15-17, 2018. I couldn't wait until the second training session. In the meantime, I kept researching the topic.

Finally, it was the day of the second training. The training was for three days—8:00 a.m. to 5:00 p.m. It started on a Tuesday and ended on a Thursday. Not a lot of people showed up for this training like the first one. I think fifty or sixty people showed up. I learned more about the topic of third-party selling. Different people gave us training on different topics. I was overwhelmed with the training. They told us it was the nature of the training. They covered many topics.

After we completed the required training, they told us to sign up for personal coaches. Personal coaches would help us with the business, as they explained. At the same time, they wanted us to open a business company like Sole Proprietorship. They promised to help us with registering as an SLC. They took all our information. In short, it required me to pay $11,000 to start the business. I refused to pay that much money because I didn't have that kind of money.

Then they advised me to apply for a credit card. So, I listened to their advice, and I opened the credit card, but the bank only gave me a $5,000 credit. But the Sellers Play Book wanted $11,000 from me. I told them that the bank only approved me for $5,000. They weren't happy with that, but at the same time, they don't want to miss the business. They signed me up for silver membership. There were three levels of membership—silver, gold, and platinum. A couple of people signed up for platinum membership. Some people signed up for gold membership. Most people signed up for silver membership. Other people refused to sign up.

At the end of the training, they took our information and gave us a badge for membership, and assigned us the coaches according to our membership level. After that day, I couldn't get hold of the guy they assigned me, but I got an email from the people who gave us the training. They promised to assign another coach. I think I sent more than one hundred emails. Finally, they assigned me one person. While I was waiting for him to start coaching me, the Federal Trade Commission announced that Sellers Play Book scammed people and was sued by the General Attorney of Minnesota.

The announcement explained how to file a lawsuit if you were affected by them. I read all the information and filed a complaint. I attached all the emails, the badge they gave us, the receipt I paid, and the bank statement. After one year, they refunded my money, including the payment I made for my credit card. Again, I wondered, was this the America I dreamed of?

Chapter Ten

Aman Come to the US

In 2018, there was political turmoil in Ethiopia, which brought about big political change. The change was due a long time ago. The system needs to change, but not the leaders. There had been mass protests, arrests, killings, and many people left the country due to political unrest. There had been protests and struggles happening for more than three decades that resulted in political change.

Oromo Protest was the main struggle organized by well-known politician Jawar Mohammed that brought change. Of course, some communities joined the struggles, like Sidama-Ejjatto, Gurage- Zarma, and Amhara-Fano. Jawar Mohammed was organizing the struggle by using social media platforms mainly

Facebook, and later, he established media called Oromia Media Network.

The current Prime Minster of Ethiopia, Dr. Abiy Ali, came into office as a result. Most of the Ethiopian diaspora community including me were happy about the change, and we supported the new government. And the new government extended his invitation to the Ethiopian diaspora community who reside abroad to come to visit his country.

Following his invitation, some of my collogues and I went to Ethiopia to show solidarity and support for the new government. At the same time, we get to see our country and witness the change. Some of my colleagues went back home for the first time since they left the country. It was so nice. Everybody looked happy about the new change. Everybody was smiling. I had missed that environment and mood. Even the neighboring country, Eritrea, had committed to bringing peace and reconciliation between Ethiopia and responding to Abiy's call. The two countries were at war for more than two decades.

Meanwhile, Aman's visa process was complete, and he was scheduled for an interview. While I was there, the American Embassy granted him a visa. So, we decided to come together to the US. It was a golden opportunity for me. I got to see him, and I got to bring him with me. I booked him a plane ticket right away. I arranged for him to be on my flight home.

OF COURSE, UNDREAMED

I left my mom and Obama together in the US, but I did shop for them for the last two weeks that I was away. And I made a taxi arrangement for Obama to go to school. After fifteen days, I came back to the US with Aman. My mom and Obama were happy for me when I brought my husband home with me. Obama was excited to see Aman again. My mom told some of my friends that I was bringing Aman with me. They threw me a welcome home party. Now, we were happy being together. The long-distance relationship had been so awful.

Even though I would have been happy to take a break from driving Uber, especially to spend time with Aman, unfortunately, I couldn't—the bills pilling up on me. So, I need to go back to it.

One night, I picked up a guy from the airport. He was going to the Happy Valley area. It was around 1:00 a.m. I was supposed to be at home this time. Aman and my mom were telling me to come home. I told them I would be home before midnight. I weren't comfortable driving to Happy Valley, but I didn't refuse the ride. I accepted and hoped that this would be my last ride. Then we drove to the destination. The guy's house was kind of uphill. I dropped him off there. Then, I needed to go down the hill. There was no turning around space in his parking lot, so I needed to back up. While I was backing up, I accidentally stepped on the gas. Then the car started accelerating down the hill. I was so freaked out; I didn't know what to do. The car hit the neighbor's mailbox and stopped. I was so disoriented. And I was scared, too. Then, right away, I changed the gear from R to D and left the spot. I put Aman on the phone on the way home in case anyone was chasing me or following me. I couldn't go to sleep the whole night thinking about the situation. I was imagining what the owner would have done if he saw me. I was feeling guilty because of leaving the spot without telling them that I hit their mailbox. I promised to go in the morning to the spot and let the owner know that it was my fault if their mailbox was damaged. I convinced myself to face the truth in the morning. I didn't tell my mom what happened.

I woke up around five a.m. and went to the location. I got there and looked around for mailbox damage, but everything looked normal. I checked it a couple of times to make sure there was no damage. I decided that I didn't need to tell the owners.

After that, I headed home and then went to sleep. When I woke up later, I saw that my car had been scrapped from the driver's side's front bumper to the driver's side's back door. It was a huge scrape. I couldn't drive with such a big scrape. So, I needed to take it to the shop. My car needed to be at the shop for a week. Due to that, I get a break and time to be with Aman.

Adjusting to life in America weren't bad for Aman because he had someone he depended on. After some time, he figured out how to get around by himself. I taught him how to do some jobs at home like cleaning, cooking, and washing dishes. In Ethiopia, most men don't do those jobs. After a couple of months, we found him a job at FedEx. Slowly and gradually, he learned things. I taught him how to drive after he got his driver's permit. He got his driver's license shortly after, and then he could do most things by himself. After that, things became easier. He encouraged me to go back to school. I told him about the lady who advised me to go back to school. He promised me to support me in everything while I was at school.

I registered at Mount Hood Community College in the Fall of 2019. In the middle of the winter term, the COVID-19 Pandemic hit the world, including the US, and everything locked down right away. No classes, no travel, no activities, no sports events. Everything was locked down. After a week of closure, the college switched many courses to remote learning. And there was an option for dropping out too, but I didn't drop out. I kept my courses. I was taking calculus, chemistry, and STAT. Those subjects were very difficult to learn remotely. Believe me, using the technology by itself was so awful and difficult, but later, I got used to it.

I stopped driving during the lockdown. Everyone was stuck at home, anyway. There weren't many activities. There was confusion, fear, and panic about the pandemic. Even the information that came from the government didn't seem to be scientifically right. The government was misleading the population about the virus itself, like using Clorox to cure it. Anyway, it was a very unfortunate time for many.

I transferred to Portland State University in the Fall of 2020. I majored in Public Health Pre-medicine. I plan to go to Medical School or Pharmacy School. That plan is on hold for the moment. I studied for two years at PSU and graduated in the Fall of 2022. Almost all my classes were remote except Genetics and World Population and Water Scarcity. I can't tell you how proud I was of myself when I took those courses in person. Being Black, African, a woman and a first-generation college student motivated me to do more and keep my focus. I accomplished my degree with honorable grades and received my certificate in the Fall of 2022.

While I was at the school, Aman was working hard. He worked twelve hours a day and seven days a week. I realized how special of a person he was. He bought us a house at the end of 2021. My son Obama and Aman always got along very well. Obama became very active and an Athlete. He played football, basketball, and track and field. He was also doing well academically too. Hopefully, his dream become true one day. Most importantly I pray for his success every second. May God accept my prayers. **AMEN!**

In Concluding, I got to a good place in life because of my perseverance, persistence, and faith in the Almighty. I never stopped moving when life became harsh and difficult.

OF COURSE, UNDREAMED

Summary by Mr. Hamza Wariyo (*Social activist, author, and entrepreneur.*)

Of Course, Undreamed is a biography of the life and challenges of Amen Mohamed and the struggles she endured in establishing a life for herself and her young son after leaving Ethiopia for a better life in America.

The book describes how complex it can be for a migrant in a new country. How she struggled with depression and self-doubt while trying to find her footing, and how finding a job with survivable income is grueling and problematic when children are involved.

It points out that as a migrant, you must adjust to massive changes in culture, language, and people's behaviors. Not having family support during difficult times and how this all affects the body and mind.

To survive, she had to work long hours and many days a week, impacting relationships and affecting her physical and mental well-being while doing her best to provide a living for herself and her son.

Community support and information sharing can be the answers to achieving well-being and working towards the goals she aimed for. Also, not everyone she interacts with is willing to help; some even put barriers in the way.

Of Course, Undreamed is a beautiful book for those

who aspire to migrate and to gain an insight into the difficulties that will be faced to achieve the outcomes for which the relocation was undertaken.